Tim Chester brings us to the foot of the cross and challenges us to live our lives from there. In his direct and yet compelling style, Chester writes with real insight and honesty into the struggles of the Christian life and with a vivid hope for its joys. He shows again and again the way in which the cross of Christ not only showers on us the grace of forgiveness but also teaches us how to live.

Dr Michael Jensen, Lecturer in Doctrine, Moore Theological College, Sydney, Australia

The Ordinary Hero is a lucid, passionate, practical guidebook that gets right to the heart of Christian discipleship. This foundational book will undoubtedly change lives.

Pete Greig, 24-7 Prayer and Alpha International

Tim Chester is rapidly becoming one of the leading young English-speaking Christian writers. His prolific work has an accessible style which has clarity and is very thought-provoking. This book is no exception. Tim encourages us to live heroic but ordinary lives that are full of the extraordinary hope that comes from believing in the death and resurrection of Jesus.

Adrian Warnock, author of Raised With Christ: How The Resurrection Changes Everything

The Ordinary Hero

The Ordinary Hero

Living the cross and resurrection

Tim Chester

INTER-VARSITY PRESS
Norton Street, Nottingham NG7 3HR, England
Email: ivp@ivpbooks.com
Website: www.ivpbooks.com

First published 2009
Reprinted 2010, 2011

British Library Cataloguing in Publication Data
A catalogue record for this book is available from the British Library.

ISBN: 978-1-84474-377-3

Set in Monotype Dante 12/15pt
Typeset in Great Britain by Servis Filmsetting Ltd, Stockport, Cheshire
Printed and bound by Ashford Colour Press Ltd, Gosport, Hampshire

Inter-Varsity Press publishes Christian books that are true to the Bible and that communicate the gospel, develop discipleship and strengthen the church for its mission in the world.

Inter-Varsity Press is closely linked with the Universities and Colleges Christian Fellowship, a student movement connecting Christian Unions in universities and colleges throughout Great Britain, and a member movement of the International Fellowship of Evangelical Students.
Website: www.uccf.org.uk

CONTENTS

FOREWORD

Just as I finished reading this excellent book, I heard that a *Coronation Street* producer, filming a wedding scene on location in a lovely fourteenth-century church, had removed a cross from the camera frame, hiding it behind some flowers. 'Nice church, shame about the cross', he implied.

As in the first century, it seems, the cross is still an embarrassment. But for the twenty-first-century Christian, I can't think of three more important words than those on the cover of this book: *cross*, *resurrection*, *living*. Far from being irrelevant to our world, the cross and resurrection speak powerfully to the deepest issues of our time.

And these three words truly belong together. Some Christians, zealous to defend the centrality of the cross, neglect the implications of the empty tomb; some Christians, rejoicing in the power of the resurrection, neglect the sufferings of Christ in which we are called to share. And many of us give lip service to both doctrines, but effectively place them in quarantine – the reality of Christ's death and resurrection barely impacts on our day-to-day lives.

This impressive book emphasizes what really matters – that the cross and resurrection are *to be lived*. And for one simple reason. Christianity is Christ. Becoming a Christian is not so much to do with a creed or a ceremony: a Christian is someone united to Jesus Christ. A church is a community where Christ is at the centre. And Christian discipleship is experiencing Christ's death and living Christ's life.

The reason why this book is so penetrating is that it constantly makes that connection. Based clearly on the Bible's teaching, Tim writes with a simplicity and directness that demonstrate how the cross and resurrection impact on every corner of my life: how they re-shape my motives and attitudes, how they call me to new ambitions, how they provoke my service, how they mould my joyful sacrifice, how they set me free to live as I should, how they encourage me to live in the light of eternal realities.

The cross and resurrection are not to be tucked away – behind the flowers, in the books of systematic theology, in the creeds or confessions. What happened that momentous weekend in Jerusalem has cosmic implications: the cross and resurrection intersect history, address our world's most troubled concerns, define the present and the future. But the cross and resurrection have radical *personal* implications: their truth is not just something to be believed, but lived.

If, like me, you are weary of a superficial Christianity, which mouths the words but fails to live the life; if, like me, you are distressed by public arguments about these doctrines, carried out in a spirit of arrogance; if, like me, you are embarrassed by the triumphalistic power language of some churches; and (most seriously) if, like me, you know that you are limping along as a follower of Christ and would dearly love to be more faithful, then these are the three words to reflect on: *cross*, *resurrection, living.*

I am convinced that, if you read each chapter slowly and prayerfully, and determine by God's Spirit to follow what the Bible teaches, you will be on track to live a life of true discipleship.

Jonathan Lamb
Langham Partnership International, Oxford, UK
February 2009

INTRODUCTION

What's really important to you? What matters? Here's God's answer to that question. 'For what I received I passed on to you as of first importance: that Christ died for our sins according to the Scriptures, that he was buried, that he was raised on the third day according to the Scriptures' (1 Corinthians 15:3–4).

This book is about what it means to follow the Christ who died and who was raised. How should the cross and resurrection shape our lives? What difference do they make on a Monday morning?

One of the phrases the New Testament often uses to describe Christians is 'in Christ' or 'united to Christ'. You and I are in Christ. This means his death is our death and his life is our life. It means his cross is our model and his resurrection is our hope.

Perhaps rather surprisingly, when the New Testament writers tell us how we should live, they don't often point back to the life of Jesus. Instead they take us again and again to the cross and resurrection. Whether they're talking about marriage or conflict or community or money or opposition or leadership or temptation or work or suffering, they look to the cross and resurrection. So if you want to know how to live as a Christian, you need to understand how the cross and resurrection shape our lives. The pattern of the cross and resurrection needs to become our reflex, our habit, our instinct. We need to live the cross and resurrection.

I've tried to write without jargon words. But there's one exception, a technical word it's very difficult to manage without: the word 'eschatology' or 'eschatological'. *Eschaton* is the Greek word for 'the last things', so 'eschatology' is the doctrine of the last things or the future age. The complication is that the last things have already begun in history with the resurrection of Jesus. We already live in the last days. Paul says we are those 'on whom the fulfilment of the ages has come' (1 Corinthians 10:11). Most Jews expected a last day, the day of the LORD, when God would intervene in history, defeat his enemies, raise the dead and vindicate his people. But with the coming of Jesus, this one event became two. Jesus has come and he is coming. The new age has begun, even as the old age continues, so that they overlap. This means the future is now and not yet. It means a past event can be 'eschatological'. The resurrection of Jesus was an eschatological event: it took place in the past, but it was also the first act of the coming age. The church is an eschatological community: we live under the reign of the coming King. We're the place on earth where the future is already taking shape. So it's an '-ology' word, but we can't really do without 'eschatology'. It's very hard to avoid it without replacing it with a couple of sentences each time. Sorry.

The death and resurrection of Jesus are the most

extraordinary events in human history. That God's promised Saviour King should die was beyond comprehension for the people of his day. It was unthinkable. That the Son of God, God incarnate, Emmanuel, God with us, should die is extraordinary. And that he should be crucified, cursed, shamed, and die under God's judgment, abandoned by the Father – for the Jews this was weakness; for the Greeks it was foolishness. Yet this is the power and wisdom of God. It's the pivot of history, the centrepiece, even the purpose of history.

And then Jesus rose again. Whoever heard of a dead man coming back to life? A dead man now living. A condemned man now vindicated. This isn't just an historical event. It's an event that pushes the boundaries of history. It signals the end of history. It's the future invading history.

But here's the point I want to make. The cross and resurrection are extraordinary events that create extraordinary lives. When we are shaped by the cross and resurrection, our ordinary lives become exceptional, special, heroic. We become ordinary heroes.

Tim Chester
January 2009

Part One:
The pardon of the cross – humble confidence

The cross is the great demonstration of God's love to us. God declares us right before him because we are in Christ. We don't need to prove ourselves because 'there is now no condemnation for those who are in Christ Jesus'. This truth gives us humble confidence. When we look into the face of God, we see a smile.

1. HOW DO YOU KNOW GOD LOVES YOU?

'God loves us.' It's a pretty foundational sort of statement for Christians. We can surround it with a lot of sentiment. We can say it rather glibly. We print it on stickers and greeting cards. Some people even say it in order to deny other truths about God: about his holiness or his anger or his justice. But it remains a great foundational truth. 'God loves us.'

But how do you know that God loves you?

Think about some possible answers.

You might say: 'I feel good today. The sun is shining. All is right with the world. *Zip-a-dee-doo-dah*. I just know that God is love.'

The problem is that tomorrow it might be raining. And tomorrow all might *not* be right with the world.

Or you might say: 'I was in a Christian meeting and as we were singing I was overcome with emotion. I felt the warmth of God's love envelop me. Tears were rolling down my cheeks. I know God loves me because I felt his love embrace me.'

That's great. It really is. But the problem is that a day may come when God seems far away. When tragedy hits your life and you pray to God, you plead with him, and you get no reply. How then will you know that God loves you?

Or you might say: 'I know God loves me because I experience his love in the love that other Christians show me. As they care for me, they show God's love to me.' Maybe during a time of difficulty, others helped you through.

That's not a bad answer. The apostle John says: 'No-one has ever seen God; but if we love one another, God lives in us and his love is made complete in us' (1 John 4:12).We do demonstrate God's love through our love for one another. The problem is that we also let one another down. There may come a time when Christians cause you pain. How then will you know that God loves you?

Or you may say: 'I know God loves me because I serve him faithfully. I live a life that pleases him.'

Serving God can certainly be thrilling. But what about when you let God down? How then will you know that he loves you? You may fear he's stopped loving you.

I'm not playing with you here. I'm not inventing hypothetical scenarios.

In 2007 violence erupted after disputed elections in Kenya. Beth, a Kenyan studying in the UK, and part of The Crowded House, the family of church planting networks to which I belong, emailed me at the time:

> This past week I've realized that I don't truly know what God being good, wise, sovereign and faithful means. I know what it doesn't mean – it doesn't mean no suffering in this life. I know that whatever he allows is for his glory and our good. But I also don't want to be flippant or simply parrot phrases as though I've merely learned them by rote. I talk to my aunt and uncle who are

doctors and have hardly slept during the last three days because of the sheer number of people coming in. I want to know what it means to talk to them and then say 'God is good'. Surely any earthly parent would come running at the sound of their baby's blood-curdling shriek. So I want to be sure I know what I mean by 'God is good' when we have prayed and prayed to the soundtrack of the screams of children being burnt, knowing that the stench is getting to heaven and silence is the response. When I watch on live television people being dragged out of cars and hacked to death, my mind spins – and not because I have wondered if God is sovereign, but because I know he is . . .

When I watch on live television people being dragged out of cars and hacked to death, my mind spins – and not because I have wondered if God is sovereign, but because I know he is . . .

Through him who loved us

I was at a conference a few years ago at which I had to share a room. One day I noticed my room-mate's Bible on his bed. There was a verse emblazoned across the front in large, brightly coloured letters: *'In all these things we are more than conquerors through him who loves us.'* That's odd, I thought to myself. I didn't think the verse went like that. So I looked it up. In his Bible. And the version on the front was wrong.

It's Romans 8:37. 'In all these things we are more than conquerors through him who loved us.' Can you spot the difference? Paul says, 'through him who love*d* us'. 'Loved' not 'loves'. Past not present tense. We might have expected him to say, 'through him who love*s* us'. Clearly the designers of that Bible expected that, because they 'corrected' Paul. But Paul says, 'through him who loved us'.

So far in Romans, Paul has been expounding the wonderful results of the work of Jesus Christ: the power of sin is broken and we've received the gift of eternal life. The problem is that Christians continue to sin, to suffer and to die. Surely these things invalidate the claims of the gospel. So in chapter 8 Paul addresses that issue head-on. He talks about:

- the presence of the Spirit: the Spirit is changing us and giving us life
- the promise of glory: present suffering will give way to future joy
- the purposes of God: God uses suffering to make us like Jesus

So, if Paul's goal was to reassure his hearers and give them confidence, surely he would stress the present reality of God's love. But Paul says 'through him who love*d* us' and he does so very deliberately. He doesn't mean that God's love has ended or run out. The point is he's referring back *to the cross*. How do we know God loves us? Because he's given us his Son. Because Jesus died for us on the cross. The cross is the great fixed, immovable declaration of God's love.

You may face suffering or hardship. You may struggle with sin in your life. You may stare death in the face. In all these things we can be confident in God's love because God so loved the world that he gave his only Son. What more could he have given? 'This is how God showed his love among us: He sent his one and only Son into the world that we might live through him. This is love: not that we loved God, but that he loved us and sent his Son as an atoning sacrifice for our sins' (1 John 4:9–10). No circumstances can change that. Christ cannot un-die for us.

In Romans 5:5 Paul says: 'Hope does not disappoint us,

because God has poured out his love into our hearts by the Holy Spirit, whom he has given us.' How does the Spirit give us this powerful experience of God's love? Is it just some precarious emotion? Paul continues, 'You see . . .' Here's the explanation of Spirit-given, heartfelt confidence in God's love. The work of the Spirit is to open our eyes to the truth. Before the Spirit we saw on the cross a weak, helpless human being dying as a pathetic failure. But now through the Spirit we see in the cross the God demonstrating his love for us:

> You see, at just the right time, when we were still powerless, Christ died for the ungodly. Very rarely will anyone die for a righteous man, though for a good man someone might possibly dare to die. But God demonstrates his own love for us in this: While we were still sinners, Christ died for us.
> (Romans 5:6–8)

What's the demonstration of God's love? The cross. How do we know God loves us? The cross. What's the basis of hope that doesn't disappoint? The cross. While 'loved' in Romans 8:37 is past tense, 'demonstrates' in 5:8 is present tense. The cross stands forever as the great demonstration of God's love.

Paul's argument begins with the question: When did Christ die for you? Was it when you started taking an interest in Jesus? Was it when you began to go to church? Was it when you cleaned up your life? Was it when you first read your Bible or prayed? No, it was when you were a sinner. When you were powerless. When you were God's enemy (10).

If God gave his Son for you when you were at your worst, what circumstances could ever make him stop loving you? If God loved us when we were his enemies, then he'll always love us. Nothing will be able to separate us from that love.

How can we know that God love*s* us? Because he love*d* us and gave his Son for us.

Beth continued her email:

> Life as I've known it has changed and will never be the way it was. And a huge chunk of me grieves . . . I'm not losing faith, for where else have I to go? Whom else have I in heaven but him? I read through Job today in one sitting and realized that Job had a lot of questions, but God didn't answer any of them. He only revealed his character and that was enough. Job says, 'I had heard of you but now I have seen you.' And so that's my prayer: that God would move me from having heard of him to seeing him, and that his comforting, sustaining and sanctifying grace would abound in the gap of hearing and seeing.

2. WILL GOD'S LOVE STAND UP IN COURT?

'Jesus loves me' is a lovely sentiment. But is it more than sentiment? Will it stand up in court? Is it robust? In the fantastical world of the film *Big Fish*, the hero, Edward Bloom, fills a field with daffodils from five states to demonstrate his love to his future wife. Is the cross just an extravagant and reckless display of love?

The problem is that, while the cross suggests that God is for me and that I'm okay with God, my life suggests I'm not okay with God. We have unfinished business. A just and holy God is surely against me since I've lived as a rebel against him. I hear his announcement of judgment. How can I also hear his declaration of love?

The truth is that the cross is more than a demonstration of love. It's love actually doing something, changing something, achieving something new. The cross gives God's love to me a legal status. It proves that he is for me, that he has made me right with him. This is love that will stand up in court.

I don't know whether you like courtroom dramas. John Gresham. Perry Mason. The defendant in the dock, the lawyers arguing out the case, the judge intervening to see fair play. The prosecution case is put. We're given flashbacks to the crime. The story is told as the trial proceeds. It's starting to look like a guilty verdict is inevitable. Everything looks cut and dried. But then the defence gets going. More flashbacks. More of the story unfolds. It's all very tense. Someone's future is at stake. Maybe even their life. The tension's rising. You're desperate to make a cup of tea, but you don't want to miss anything. And then, at the last minute, there's a twist and the whole situation changes.

Now imagine just such a scenario, but this time you're in the dock. The case against you is made. The case for you is put. Witnesses are cross-examined. All the same tension is there, only this time more so. This time it's your future that's at stake. God says that one day there's going to be just such a court case. And this is no TV fiction. This is for real. And in the dock will be humanity – you and I. 'This will take place on the day when God will judge men's secrets through Jesus Christ, as my gospel declares' (Romans 2:16).

The defence case: 'I acted in ignorance'

The charge against us is nothing less than treason against God and his good, loving rule. And God's verdict is anticipated as he hands us over to our evil ways (Romans 1:18, 24, 26, 28).

But is it fair? Is the verdict going to be just? Is God righteous? That's the issue. So in Romans 1 – 3 Paul reviews the case. He examines the evidence. He allows the defence to put its case. He retells the story. You've got to imagine our TV courtroom drama full of flashbacks. Paul switches between the courtroom and the story.

At first we plead ignorance. 'I didn't know there was a God. I didn't know what he expected of me.' So Paul gives us our first flashback to the story. He takes us back to the beginning. God made a good world. He made us to know him. His reign was a reign of life, freedom, blessing and peace. He made a world in which his existence and lordship could be known. 'God has made it plain . . . his eternal power and divine nature have been clearly seen' (1:19–20).

But then we move on to the next flashback. It takes us to the garden of Eden. There the first man and woman doubted God's word and rejected God's rule. It's a story that's been repeated over and over again. You and I decide we want to be god of our own lives. We live without God. And so people 'suppress the truth by their wickedness' (1:18). We don't want to live in obedience to God and so we reject the knowledge of God (1:25). It's not that we can't know; it's that we refuse to know God. The result is that we live in defiance of God, spreading pain and suffering (1:26–32).

The defence case: 'I'm a good person'

The defence lawyer stands up again. 'Yes, yes,' he says, 'so true. How dreadful. But my client isn't like that. She's a respectable woman. He passes judgment on those other sorts of people' (2:1).

But the prosecution declares: 'Because of your stubbornness and your unrepentant heart, you are storing up wrath against yourself for the day of God's wrath, when his righteous judgment will be revealed' (2:5). What is judged is not outward respectability, but our hearts. Jesus the Judge is going to expose our secrets (2:16). He's going to judge the desire in all of us to be god of own lives. 'I lived a good life' will be no excuse because it won't stand up in the court. The evidence won't support it.

As far as the story is concerned, there's a bit of a lull. It looks as if nothing is happening. But Paul says God is waiting. 'Do you show contempt for the riches of his kindness, tolerance and patience, not realising that God's kindness leads you towards repentance?' (2:4). There's a pause in the story because God is being patient, giving humanity every chance to turn back to him.

The defence case: 'I'm a religious person'

The defence case takes a different line. The argument this time is one for Jews only: 'We have the law' (2:17–18). This isn't the previous defence argument rehashed. It's not: 'I *keep* the law.' No, the argument is: 'I *have* the law.' In other words, 'I'm part of God's chosen people. I have a relationship with God. God is on my side.' It's an argument to make the Jews a special case, though plenty of other people do their own version of it: 'I may not be perfect, but I do go to church; I'm part of a Christian family; I live in a Christian country.'

And so we get another flashback in the story. The next thing that happens in the story is that God chooses a man called Abraham. He promises him a people who will be God's people. And God did create a people as he promised – the people of Israel. He rescued them from slavery in Egypt and brought them into a good land.

They were picked out *for* the nations. God said to Abraham: 'I will bless those who bless you, and whoever curses you I will curse; and all peoples on earth will be blessed through you' (Genesis 12:3). The people of Israel were to be a light to the nations. This was the beginning of God's solution to humanity's plight: a nation who would so live under God's reign that people would be attracted to him. They would see it was good to live under God's reign. They would come back to him. God sent his spokesmen, the prophets, to inspire the people with that vision. They speak of the nations flooding to Israel to worship God (Isaiah 2:1–5).

But what happened? Israel rejected God. Instead of being a light to the nations, they became like the nations. They followed their evil ways. The solution become part of the problem (Romans 2:17–29). They didn't lead the nations to God. Quite the opposite: 'As it is written: "God's name is blasphemed among the Gentiles because of you"' (2:24). They actually brought God's name into disrepute! So it's not being ethnically Jewish that counts, but an inward transformation that God brings about by his Spirit (2:28–29). Being Jewish or religious or attending church is no defence if that inward change hasn't taken place.

The verdict: guilty!

And so we come to the verdict: 'What shall we conclude then? Are we any better? Not at all! We have already made the charge that Jews and Gentiles alike are all under sin' (3:9).

But we're not quite done with the evidence yet. One more witness is called. The defendants 'rely on the law' so let the law take the stand. What does it say? Romans 3:10–18 provides quote after quote from the Old Testament. The message? Guilty, guilty, guilty. Here's a dramatic twist in the drama. The defence witness turns out to support the prosecution case.

And so the final verdict is: 'Now we know that whatever the law says, it says to those who are under the law [i.e. to Jews], so that every mouth may be silenced and the whole world [i.e. both Jew and Gentile] held accountable to God. Therefore no-one will be declared righteous in his sight by observing the law; rather, through the law we become conscious of sin' (3:19–20).

We're all accountable to God and we're all guilty.

But neither the trial, nor the story are quite over. There's one more scene in each case. Another development in the story. Another twist in the trial.

The climax of the story: Jesus Christ is the faithful one who sets us free

In Romans 3:1–4 Paul raises an important question: Does Israel's unfaithfulness mean that God's plan is wrecked? If the solution became the problem, then is there any solution at all? Has God proved unfaithful to his promises?

And the answer must be: Yes, God's plan has failed *unless* a faithful Israelite can be found who will fulfil God's promises. What we need is one faithful person who can represent Israel and humanity. And with that question in mind, we get our final flashback:

> But now a righteousness from God, apart from law, has been made known, to which the Law and the Prophets testify. This righteousness from God comes through faith in Jesus Christ to all who believe. There is no difference, for all have sinned and fall short of the glory of God, and are justified freely by his grace through the redemption that came by Christ Jesus.
> (Romans 3:21–24)

'Through faith in Jesus Christ' in verse 22 is better translated 'through the faithfulness of Jesus Christ'. (The original Greek can mean either, and 'through faith' would be unnecessary since the next thing Paul says is that this comes 'to all who believe'.) God is faithful to his plan through the faithfulness of Jesus. Through Jesus, God makes known his 'righteousness' – his faithfulness to his covenant promises (doing right by his word, as it were). Jesus is the one faithful Israelite who makes God known to the world.

And he redeems us just as God redeemed Israel from slavery and death in Egypt (3:23–24). Many years before Christ, the Israelites had been rescued from Egyptian slavery after God inflicted an angel of death on Egypt. The Israelites escaped because the angel of death passed over every home daubed with the blood of sacrifice. Paul says that this was a picture of what Jesus Christ does. By setting us free from slavery to sin, he sets us free from death through his sacrifice. *The climax of the story is that God is righteous in the sense that he is true to his promise to save those who have faith in Jesus Christ.* Through the faithfulness of Jesus Christ, God *does* create a people who are his people.

The climax of the trial: Jesus Christ takes our punishment

> God presented him as a sacrifice of atonement, through faith in his blood. He did this to demonstrate his justice, because in his forbearance he had left the sins committed beforehand unpunished – he did it to demonstrate his justice at the present time, so as to be just and the one who justifies those who have faith in Jesus.
> (Romans 3:25–26)

The accusation has been made. The evidence has been examined. The story has been told. The witnesses have been heard. The verdict has been passed. All have sinned. And now the judgment falls. But what a twist! For it falls on Christ instead of us. The phrase 'sacrifice of atonement' here means a sacrifice that turns away anger. In other words, God's judgment has been redirected away from us and onto Jesus. It falls in the middle of history on the cross, instead of at the end of history on you and me.

And so God forgives those who have faith in Christ. He forgives and still is righteous. *The climax of the court case is that God is righteous in the sense that he is just when he acquits those who have faith in Christ.* The Judge acts justly – he condemns evil. But by condemning sin in Christ we can go free. We can be declared 'Not guilty':

> Therefore, there is now no condemnation for those who are in Christ Jesus, because through Christ Jesus the law of the Spirit of life set me free from the law of sin and death. For what the law was powerless to do in that it was weakened by the sinful nature, God did by sending his own Son in the likeness of sinful man to be a sin offering. And so he condemned sin in sinful man, in order that the righteous requirements of the law might be fully met in us, who do not live according to the sinful nature but according to the Spirit.
> (Romans 8:1–4)

Jesus the sinless one became 'in the likeness of sinful man'. In other words, God treated him as a sinful man. He became a sin offering. In the Old Testament people symbolically placed their sin on an animal and the animal was then killed. The animal took the penalty for sin which was death. It was an illustration. Jesus is the real thing. God placed your sin and my sin on Jesus. He bore your punishment and my punishment. He died your death and my death. God condemned sin in Jesus. The result? Condemnation for Jesus. No condemnation for us. A swap. A great exchange. The result? 'Therefore, there is now no condemnation for those who are in Christ Jesus.'

By faith we're united with Jesus. We become 'those who

are in Christ Jesus'. This means his death is my death. His life is my life. His vindication is my vindication. His righteousness is my righteousness. God counts me righteous in Christ. In his love he declares that he is for me and that declaration has legal status.

3. HUMILITY

The pardon of the cross creates a humble confidence in those who believe. Humble confidence might sound like a contradiction. Like warm ice. Or a desert that blooms. But our humility and our confidence are looking in different directions.

Our confidence comes when we look to God in the light of the cross. We see in the cross God's great declaration of his love to us and the legal status of that love. We discover that there is now no condemnation for those who are in Christ Jesus. And that gives us confidence in the face of sin, suffering and death. Indeed it's this confidence that enables us to be humble because we don't need to assert ourselves.

Meanwhile, humility comes when we look at ourselves in the light of the cross. There we discover that we're rebels against God. When we get the chance, we murder our Creator. That's what we are like. We discover our desperate need for grace. We're humbled. So when we see a messed-up, struggling person we don't see someone inferior. We see ourselves. We see a sinner like us in desperate need of God's grace.

The most widely-known Bible verse in the United States is: 'God helps those who help themselves.'[1] The tragic irony, of course, is that this isn't from the Bible at all. Instead, the Bible says God helps those who humble themselves (James 4:6, 10). Isaiah says that 'the high and lofty One' lives, not with people who are high and lofty, but with the 'contrite and lowly in spirit' (Isaiah 57:15).

Consider the effect on a culture of the proclamation that God helps those who help themselves. Such a culture will see prosperity as a reward for self-attainment. 'Wealth is my achievement,' people will suppose. 'I deserve it and it entails no moral responsibility towards those who don't deserve it. The poor must be at fault in some way, receiving a just outcome for their fecklessness which I've escaped as a result of my virtue.' Back in the sixth century, Gregory the Great said, 'Belief in inequality arises from the spring of pride.'[2] In other words, people justify inequality by reasoning that their wealth and privileges arise from some kind of superiority – whether in skills, experience, entrepreneurial drive or national character.

But the blessings that the prosperous enjoy are a generous gift from God. Paul's 'evangelistic pitch' in Lystra was to invite his hearers to acknowledge the God who shows 'kindness by giving you rain from heaven and crops in their seasons; he provides you with plenty of food and fills your hearts with joy' (Acts 14:17). Our upbringing, education and intelligence shouldn't make us feel superior; they should make us grateful. And never far behind true gratitude are her sister virtues: generosity and humility.

In Romans 1 – 3 we saw how we've been caught up in

a legal drama that ends with our acquittal. What happens when we walk out of the court as free people?

The Bible tells us what ought to happen: 'Where, then, is boasting? It is excluded. On what principle? On that of observing the law? No, but on that of faith' (3:27). Paul imagines a Jew boasting that he has the law of Moses or that he's part of God's chosen people. But the law doesn't save us. Indeed the law could only condemn us. Jews are just as bad as Gentiles. And in case Gentiles get uppity, Paul later warns Gentiles not to boast (11:11–16). 'There is no difference, for all have sinned and fall short of the glory of God, and are justified freely by his grace through the redemption that came by Christ Jesus' (3:22–24). We're all sinners. No-one can get superior. No-one can get proud. We're all saved by God's gracious, unmerited love. We're all saved by the work of Jesus. That's why what counts is faith in Jesus. And we can't even claim the credit for our faith because it too is a gift from God (Ephesians 2:8–9).

'All of you, clothe yourselves with humility towards one another,' says Peter, 'because "God opposes the proud but gives grace to the humble"' (1 Peter 5:5.) It may well be that Peter had in mind the example of Jesus on the night before he died. John 13 describes how Jesus 'got up from the meal, took off his outer clothing, and wrapped a towel round his waist' (4). He clothed himself with the apron of humility. And then 'he poured water into a basin and began to wash his disciples' feet' (5). While we vie for positions of honour, Jesus is wearing an apron. While we pursue power and cling to authority, Jesus is among us as one who serves. While we compete for publicity or esteem, Jesus is at our feet.

But the example of Jesus isn't enough. On its own, it creates an unattainable model. Worse still, it can be self-defeating. In *The Screwtape Letters*, C. S. Lewis creates a fictional correspondence between two demons outlining the strategies to be employed to harm a young Christian man, their 'patient'.

> Your patient has become humble; have you drawn his attention to the fact? All virtues are less formidable to us once the man is aware that he has them, but this is especially true of humility. Catch him at the moment when he is really poor in spirit and smuggle into his mind the gratifying reflection, 'By jove! I'm being humble,' and almost immediately pride – pride at his own humility – will appear. If he awakes to the danger and tries to smother this new form of pride, make him proud of his attempt – and so on, through as many stages as you please. But don't try this too long, for fear you awake his sense of humour and proportion, in which case he will merely laugh at you and go to bed.[3]

Humility can't be *achieved*! Lewis goes on to define humility as self-forgetfulness. When you meet a humble person, you don't leave them and think, 'What a humble person.' You leave thinking, 'That person was really interested in me.' Humility is not falsely thinking our abilities are less valuable than they really are – 'clever men trying to believe they are fools'.[4] Humility is self-forgetfulness and so it will never be attained through continual self-monitoring. But if humility is self-forgetfulness, how then are we to remember to forget ourselves?

The great English Puritan John Owen may help us. He said: 'There are two things that are suited to humble the souls of men, and they are, first, a due consideration of God, and then of themselves – of God, in his greatness, glory, holiness, power, majesty, and authority; of ourselves, in our mean, abject, and sinful condition.'[5]

The glory of God

Humility begins with a vision of God and his glory. We remember our place in the universe. We were made for God's glory. He, and not I, is the Almighty, the Holy One, the Creator, robed in splendour. He, and not I, is central and sovereign. Theologians talk about God's incommunicable attributes. We can reflect (albeit very imperfectly) some of God's attributes: God is love and we can be loving. God is holy and we can be holy. But God's incommunicable attributes are those things about God which we can never share, not even in part. His eternity. His unchanging character. His presence everywhere. God is radically different from us. We're merely creatures – and sinful, rebellious creatures at that. In Isaiah 66:1–2 the LORD proclaims his glory: 'Heaven is my throne, and the earth is my footstool.' He doesn't depend on humanity in any way: 'Where is the house you will build for me? Where will my resting place be? Has not my hand made all these things, and so they came into being?' But he continues, 'This is the one I esteem: he who is humble and contrite in spirit, and trembles at my word.'

The cross of Jesus

The life of Jesus provides a wonderful model of humility to follow. But if we want to be humble, we must move from looking at the life of Jesus to looking at the cross of Jesus. His life shows us humility; his cross humbles us. It's at the cross that we see ourselves as we really are. Here are two quotes from the two 'greats' (in the spirit of Mark 10:43) of twentieth-century British evangelicalism: Martyn Lloyd-Jones and John Stott:

> There is only one thing I know of that crushes me to the ground and humiliates me to the dust, and that is to look at the Son of God, and especially contemplate the cross . . . Nothing else can

> do it. When I see that I am a sinner . . . that nothing but the Son of God on the cross can save me, I'm humbled to the dust . . . Nothing but the cross can give us this spirit of humility.[6]

> The cross tells us some very unpalatable truths about ourselves, namely that we are sinners under the righteous curse of God's law and we cannot save ourselves . . . If we could have been forgiven by our good works . . . we may be quite sure that there would have been no cross. Every time we look at the cross, Christ seems to be saying to us, 'I am here because of you. It is your sin I am bearing, your curse I am suffering, your death I am dying.' Nothing in history or in the universe cuts us down to size like the cross. All of us have inflated views of ourselves, especially in self-righteousness, until we have visited a place called Calvary. It is there, at the foot of the cross, that we shrink to our true size.[7]

The secret of humility is never to stray far from the cross. It should often be in our thoughts, often on our lips, often in our songs, determining our actions, shaping our attitudes, captivating our affections. This is why the remembrance of the Lord's death in communion is so integral to Christian spirituality.

The secret of humility is never to stray far from the cross. It should often be in our thoughts, often on our lips, often in our songs, determining our actions, shaping our attitudes, captivating our affections.

The cross gives us a right view of ourselves. The cross gives us a proper estimation of ourselves. Our righteousness is unmerited. Our status is unearned. What we bring is our sin and shame. What we receive is an inheritance of glory. Everything we have and everything we are is the result of God's grace. So the cross keeps us humble.

The cross gives us a right view of other people. Grace is a great leveller. If my righteousness is unmerited and my achievements are God's work in me, then I can't claim any superiority. I can't look down on other people. And so Paul says: 'Accept one another, then, just as Christ accepted you, in order to bring praise to God' (Romans 15:7).

The cross subverts all human notions of glory. The message we proclaim – the message of Christ crucified – is foolishness and weakness in the sight of the world. 'We preach Christ crucified, a stumbling-block to Jews and foolishness to Gentiles, but to those who are called, both Jews and Greeks, [the proclamation of Christ crucified] is Christ the power of God and the wisdom of God. For the foolishness of God is wiser than man's wisdom, and the weakness of God is stronger than man's strength' (1 Corinthians 1:23–25).

And with this foolish, weak message of the cross goes a foolish, weak community of the cross. 'But God chose the foolish things of the world to shame the wise; God chose the weak things of the world to shame the strong; He chose the lowly things of this world and the despised things – and the things that are not – to nullify the things that are, so that no-one may boast before him' (27–29).

The cross leaves no scope for human boasting. Instead our one boast is in Christ Jesus, 'who has become for us wisdom from God – that is, our righteousness, holiness and redemption. Therefore . . . "Let him who boasts boast in the Lord"' (30–31).

We need to ditch our worldly notions of success. We need to ditch our preoccupation with numbers and size. We need to turn our notions of success upside down so that we align them with God's kingdom perspective (Mark 4:26–32).

4. CONFIDENCE

'There is now no condemnation.' If only we could believe this, Christians need never feel condemned.

Pride arises when we think we're good enough for God or better than other people. The cross gives us a realistic view of ourselves. But many of us have the opposite problem. We think we're not good enough for God. And, of course, in and of ourselves we could never be good enough for God. But God sees us in Christ. When he looks on you, he sees you in Christ with the righteousness of Christ. And so we're accepted. There is now no condemnation.

Think about those challenging Bible studies you've heard. The times your sins have been exposed. The times when you've failed in your duties. There is now no condemnation. Your sins are real sins. They grieve the heart of God. They rob God of his glory. They should grieve your heart too. But there is now no condemnation. You're free. God regards you as righteous. And so should you. You should think of yourself as a saint, a child of God, an heir of glory. On the cross God reveals the full extent of our sin at the very moment at which he also reveals the full extent of his grace. You should come before God with confidence and freedom. God doesn't merely tolerate you. In Christ he smiles upon you as a Father. Terry Virgo says:

> If you are not thoroughly persuaded that God has given you a gift of righteousness that makes you thoroughly acceptable to God, you will constantly be battling with a general sense of disqualification and guilt. You will fear that you are not sanctified enough to be acceptable to God and this is where you will make a huge mistake . . . God has justified you freely! He has given you thorough acceptance in his sight, not because of your changed life but because of his good pleasure in giving you the very righteousness of Christ.[8]

There's no need to earn approval, no need to prove yourself, no need to perform. It isn't just about what happens on the day of judgment. Many Christians believe they'll be acquitted on the last day through the blood of Jesus. But they never apply this great truth to the next day. They sing it on Sunday mornings, but they don't live it on Monday mornings. Instead, we try to prove ourselves through our work or our performance or our morality or our success or our service. But the work of proving yourself or justifying yourself has all been done by Christ. 'It is finished.' Don't rob Christ of his glory by treating his work as inadequate. Glorify him by resting and relying wholly on his cross. Relax. Enjoy. Rest. Hear him say: 'Come to me, all you who are weary and burdened, and I will give you rest' (Matthew 11:28).

Accepted and accepting

The Bible often links our attitude to God with our attitude to other people. So Jesus, for example, says: 'If you forgive men when they sin against you, your heavenly Father will also forgive you. But if you do not forgive men their sins, your Father will not forgive your sins' (Matthew 6:14–15). We don't earn forgiveness from God by forgiving other people. Rather, our attitude to others reveals our attitude to God. In this case, giving people what they deserve (= not forgiving) shows that we (wrongly) think we get what we deserve from God.

We don't often see it this way because we leave God out of the picture. I may say, 'I'm angry because my life is a mess.' But what I'm really saying is, 'I'm angry with God because God has let my life be a mess.'

This principle can help test how much we really believe there is no condemnation in our hearts in the day to day.

- If you're angry for ill-defined reasons or often angry, it may well be because you feel angry towards God (even if you don't think of it like that) because you view life as a contract in which God hasn't kept his side of the bargain.
- If you feel condemned by other people or judged by them, it may be because you feel condemned by God because you haven't embraced the wonderful truth that there is now no condemnation for those who are in Christ Jesus.
- If you're indifferent towards people, it may be because you're indifferent towards God because you haven't had God's love poured out in your heart.
- If you're insecure, often worried about what people think, always keen to prove yourself, unwilling to let

an argument go, then that's a good sign that you're desperate to prove yourself because you've not grasped God's grace to you: the no-condemnation of the gospel.

On the other hand:

- If you're confident that God loves you, then you'll love other people.
- If you're confident that God's accepted you, then you'll accept other people.
- If you're confident that God died for you, then you'll lay down your life for other people.
- If you're confident that God loved you while you were still his enemy, then you'll not complain when other people let you down.
- If you're confident that God's gracious to you, then you'll be gracious to other people.

The point is not to stop being angry or insecure or uncaring. The point is to believe there is no condemnation. 'The cross is the blazing fire at which the flame of our love is kindled, but we have to get near enough *to it* for its sparks to fall on us.'[9]

Who can be against us?

In Romans 8, Paul emphasizes the certainty and surety of God's love by asking a series of questions.

1. Who can be against us?

'If God is for us, who can be against us?' (31–32). Paul answers this first question with another question, but it's a rhetorical question, a question which is really an answer. 'He who did not spare his own Son, but gave him up for us all – how will he not also, along with him, graciously give us all things?'

(32). In other words, why should we think that God would abandon us when he's already given us his Son? Why should we think there's any limit to his love when he's already given what was most precious to him? People may oppose us, people may be against us, but they can't overturn or overcome God's love for us.

2. Who will bring any charge?

'Who will bring any charge against those whom God has chosen?' (33). You might say, 'The problem is not other people (being against me), the problem is me and my sin. I'm the one who can separate me from God's love. I keep on sinning. Surely I've cut myself off from God.'

And what's Paul's response? 'It is God who justifies' (33). You're not made right with God by what you do. You don't *do* it in the first place, so why suppose you could *undo* it! Did God love you and justify you because you were so good? Of course not. He loved you when you were his enemy. You were powerless to justify yourself and now you're powerless to un-justify yourself! Perhaps this is the ultimate humiliation. Not only can we not contribute to our salvation; we can't even wreck our salvation. But who cares? This is our great hope, our great confidence, our great assurance.

3. Who is he that condemns?

'Who is he that condemns?' (34) What if someone else should bring a charge against me that I couldn't answer? Well, argues Paul, think about it. Who could rightly condemn us? There's only one person and that's Jesus. 'Christ Jesus, who died – more than that, who was raised to life – is at the right hand of God and is also interceding for us' (34). The only One who could condemn us is the One who died for us. The Judge who could condemn is the Saviour who rose so that we might be justified. The One who could accuse is the One who intercedes for us.

4. Who shall separate us?

'Who shall separate us from the love of Christ? Shall trouble or hardship or persecution or famine or nakedness or danger or sword? As it is written: "For your sake we face death all day long; we are considered as sheep to be slaughtered." No, in all these things we are more than conquerors through him who loved us' (35–37).

Can anything separate us from God's love?

Sin can't separate us from God's love – God first loved us when we were sinners. Christ covers our sin and he intercedes for us.

Suffering can't separate us from God's love. No matter what we go through, God is with us. Suffering isn't a sign that he no longer loves us; it's a sign that God's promised new world hasn't yet come.

Even *death* can't separate us from God's love. Death might look like the limit of God's love. But for Christians death is the beginning of a much closer and more intimate relationship with God.

And so Paul concludes: 'For I am convinced that neither death nor life, neither angels nor demons, neither the present nor the future, nor any powers, neither height nor depth, nor anything else in all creation, will be able to separate us from the love of God that is in Christ Jesus our Lord' (38–39).

The Father's smile

Our heavenly Father is not a stern father who needs to be placated by his Son. Maybe your human father was like that. Stern. Distant. Maybe you approached him hesitantly or reluctantly. But your divine Father isn't like that. The Son's actions are the outflow of the Father's love. Please get that right. The Son didn't placate God to make him favourably disposed to us. No, it's the other way round. The work of the Son starts with the love of the Father. John Owen says:

> Jesus Christ is the beam of his Father's love and through him the Father's love reaches down and touches us.
>
> It is God's will that he should always be seen as gentle, kind, tender, loving and unchangeable. It is his will that we see him as the Father, and the great fountain and reservoir of all grace and love . . . Believers learn that it was God's will and purpose to love them from everlasting to everlasting in Christ, and that all reason for God to be angry with us and treat us as his enemies has been taken away. The believer, being brought by Christ into the bosom of the Father, rests in the full assurance of God's love and of never being separated from that love.
>
> Many saints have no greater burden in their lives than that their hearts do not constantly delight and rejoice in God. There is still in them a resistance to walking close with God . . . So do this: set your thoughts on the eternal love of the Father and see if your heart is not aroused to delight in him. Sit down for a while at this delightful spring of living water and you will soon find its streams sweet and delightful. You who used to run from God will not now be able, even for a second, to keep at any distance from him.[10]

God doesn't merely tolerate us. He delights in us. We make him sing for joy. 'The LORD your God is with you, he is mighty to save. He will take great delight in you, he will quiet you with his love, he will rejoice over you with singing' (Zephaniah 3:17).

God doesn't merely tolerate us. He delights in us. We make him sing for joy.

I love my family. But some days, I wake up in a grumpy mood and everything they do seems to irritate me. God never wakes up in a grumpy mood. 'Because of the LORD's great love we are not consumed, for his compassions never fail. They are new every morning; great is your faithfulness' (Lamentations 3:22–23). I never need to wake up worrying what mood God might be in. Every morning without fail he is merciful and compassionate. 'From everlasting to everlasting the Lord's love is with those who fear him' (Psalm 103:17). There'll never come a day when God stops loving his people. He'll never change his mind. Never give up on us. 'His love endures for ever,' says Psalm 136. But we're prone to forget this in the pressures of life so the Psalm repeats it. Twenty-six times. 'His love endures for ever . . . His love endures for ever . . . His love endures for ever . . .'

The film *Notting Hill* famously tells the story of a glamorous movie star, Anna Scott, played by Julia Roberts, who falls in love with William Thacker, a humble bookshop owner played by Hugh Grant. Towards the end of the film, William rushes across London to ask Anna to stay with him in England, arriving in the middle of her press conference. At the climax of the film, her face breaks into a smile. We see her smile flash up on TV monitor after TV monitor. When you see that smile, your heart melts, the tension relaxes, the story resolves, everything is now right.

When you look into the face of God, what do you see? Do you see a frown? Do you see a judge? A schoolmaster? Or do you see a smile?

In Christ, God smiles upon us. Who can resist that smile?

Part Two:
The practice of the cross – sacrificial service

Jesus says that anyone who wants to follow him must take up their cross. Our model is the sacrificial love, service and suffering that we see in the cross. The way of the cross covers every area of life from martyrdom to everyday self-denial. In this way, we show the value of Christ and find true joy.

5. THE WAY OF JESUS = THE WAY OF THE CROSS

The Bible says we're to be 'imitators' of Jesus (1 Thessalonians 1:6). God's great purpose in our life is that we might 'be conformed to the likeness of his Son' (Romans 8:29). We're told, 'Clothe yourselves with the Lord Jesus Christ' (Romans 13:14).

But what does it mean to imitate Jesus?

Clearly we're not to imitate Jesus in every respect. On one hand, he was an unmarried Jewish male and an itinerant preacher in first-century rural Palestine. On the other hand, he was the Son of God, who accomplished the salvation of the world. We can't imitate the specifics of his humanity and we certainly can't imitate his divine nature and saving role. So what exactly does it mean to follow Jesus?

This is how Jesus answered that question: '*If anyone would come after me, he must deny himself and take up his cross daily and follow me*' (Luke 9:23). Following Jesus means following the way of the cross. Later, in Luke's Gospel, Jesus says: 'And anyone who does not carry his cross and follow me cannot be my disciple' (Luke 14:27).

It's a call to die. For some, this may mean a call to a literal death – to persecution and martyrdom. For us in the West, the reality of the call to die is distant. But reality it is. Even in our context, converts to Christianity from a Muslim background have received threatening phone calls. They weigh up baptism carefully, knowing the possible consequences. So for some, the way of the cross will prove to be a call to martyrdom.

But for all of us, it's a call to die to self. This way of the cross isn't the calling of a few. It's the stamp of every Christian's life. When Paul says we're to be imitators of God, he spells this out by saying that we're to 'live a life of love, just as Christ loved us and gave himself up for us as a fragrant offering and sacrifice to God' (Ephesians 5:1–2).

To follow the way of the cross means to show the same sacrificial love that Jesus showed when he went to the cross. The same self-denial. The same submission to God. The same willingness to suffer. The same service of others. Here are the five Ss that I think describe what it means to take up your cross daily:

- sacrifice
- submission
- self-denial
- service
- suffering

They overlap to create a picture of the attitudes and actions that characterize the way of the cross. 'Cruciformity,' Michael Gorman calls it. Conformed to the cross. He summarizes it as 'sacrificial love . . . self-giving love . . . status-renouncing love'.[11] This is what it means to follow Jesus.

Everywhere we look in the New Testament, the pattern is the same: we're called to follow the way of the cross.

Jesus: 'he must deny himself and take up his cross and follow me'

We've already seen that this is how Jesus defined discipleship: 'If anyone would come after me, he must deny himself and take up his cross and follow me' (Mark 8:34; see also Matthew 16:24–28; Luke 9:23–27). In Mark's Gospel this saying kicks off a section in which Jesus talks about what it means to be a disciple as he and the disciples journey together towards Jerusalem (8:27 – 10:45). There's a parallel between the way to Jerusalem (the way *to* the cross) and the way of discipleship (the way *of* the cross). Mark has built this teaching on discipleship around three predictions by Jesus of his sufferings and death (8:31; 9:31; 10:33–34). Jesus links discipleship – taking up one's cross – with his own cross.

Where does this focus on the cross leave the teaching of Jesus? The answer is that the cross is the world's response to his teaching. The primary answer to the question 'Why did Jesus die?' is of course that he died as the culmination of the divine plan of salvation (Acts 4:27–28). Jesus died to reconcile us to God. But this doesn't rule out another answer which is that Jesus died because his words and actions challenged the interests and ideology of those in power. The Jewish leaders and Roman authorities didn't kill Jesus because they wanted to fulfil God's plan. They killed Jesus because he was countercultural, anti-establishment, socially subversive. Jesus himself explicitly aligned himself with God's prophets whose proclamation, throughout history, of a coming new world order had been suppressed (Mark 12:1–12; Luke 11:47–51). And he warned his followers that they, too, would be rejected like the prophets as they lived his new way of life as part of his new community (Matthew 5:11–12). The cross is the sign that the teachings of Jesus have no place in a self-centred, self-righteous, self-serving world. But his teachings do take shape in the community of the cross.

> As Jesus demonstrated, the world, for all its beauty, is hostile to the truth. Witness without compromise leads to worldly hostility. The cross is not a sign of the church's quiet, suffering submission to the powers-that-be, but rather the church's revolutionary participation in the victory of Christ over those powers . . . The cross is a sign of what happens when one takes God's account of reality more seriously that Caesar's.[12]

Paul: 'the fellowship of sharing in his sufferings, becoming like him in his death'

Suffering was written into Paul's call. Paul first encountered the Risen Christ on the road to Damascus, discovering that the Jesus whose followers he was persecuting is the Lord. What's the next thing he needs to know? Mission and suffering: 'The Lord said to Ananias, "Go! This man is my chosen instrument to carry my name before the Gentiles and their kings and before the people of Israel. I will show him how much he must suffer for my name"' (Acts 9:15–16).

Paul speaks of Christians sharing in Christ's sufferings. 'Now if we are children, then we are heirs – heirs of God and co-heirs with Christ, if indeed we share in his sufferings in order that we may also share in his glory' (Romans 8:17). Certainly this involves the possibility of persecution. But the way of the cross is more than that. It forms the heart of Paul's teaching on the Christian life. In urging Christians to give generously, Paul points to the cross (2 Corinthians 8:9). Our attitude to those with weak consciences is to be governed by Christ's example

(Romans 14:15; 15:1–7; see also 1 Corinthians 10:31 – 11:1). Husbands are told to love their wives just as Christ loved the church and gave himself up for her (Ephesians 5:25). Whether the subject is giving, relationships within the church, or marriage, the cross forms the basis of Paul's teaching.

Paul saw his own ministry as a participation in the sufferings of Christ. He speaks of wanting to know 'the fellowship of sharing in [Christ's] sufferings, becoming like him in his death' (Philippians 3:10). He labours to the extent that he is 'being poured out like a drink offering' (Philippians 2:17). The sufferings of Christ 'flow over into our lives' (2 Corinthians 1:5); sufferings shared by the Corinthians (2 Corinthians 1:6–7) and Philippians (Philippians 1:29–30). In his love for the Thessalonians, he shared with them not only the gospel but his life as well (1 Thessalonians 2:7–8). Although such cross-centred living often involved persecution and imprisonment for Paul, it's clear that it was more than this: it was the sacrificial giving of himself in the service of others. Paul often calls himself a 'slave' to Christ – a person with no rights. When Paul feels the need to accredit his ministry to the church in Corinth he doesn't do it by listing his successes, but with a litany of his sufferings and difficulties (1 Corinthians 4:8–17; 2 Corinthians 6:3–10; 11:21 – 12:10).

In Galatians 6, Paul says: 'I bear on my body the marks of Jesus' (17). He wasn't coming over all mystical. He could literally pull up his clothing and show you the marks of Christ – the scars from the lashes he'd received. They showed he was united with Christ. They showed he was a true servant of Jesus. Michael Gorman concludes: 'Paul wanted his life and ministry to tell a story; a story that corresponded to the "story of the cross," to his gospel. His spirituality was therefore a *narrative* spirituality, an experience of re-presenting in living form the word of the cross.'[13]

Peter: 'to this you were called, because Christ suffered for you, leaving you an example'

The pattern is similar in Peter's first epistle. Peter urges his readers, in the light of their status as the new people of God, to 'live such good lives among the pagans that, though they accuse you of doing wrong, they may see your good deeds and glorify God on the day he visits us' (2:11–12). He then applies this to subjects of the state (2:13–17); slaves (2:18–21); wives – particularly wives of unbelieving husbands (3:1–6); husbands (3:7) and 'finally' within the Christian community (3:8–12). The section begins and ends with the possibility of suffering for doing good (2:12; 3:13–18) and this theme runs throughout (2:14–16; 2:19–20; 3:1–2; 3:9). The sections on subjects, slaves and wives all begin in the same way: 'submit yourselves'. At the centre of this exhortation is the example of Christ (2:21–25). In 2:21 Peter says Christians were called to 'suffer for doing good' (2:20). Why? 'For to this you have been called, because Christ also suffered for you, leaving you an example, so that you might follow in his steps' (1 Peter 2:21 ESV).

Peter highlights two things about Christ's sufferings.

First, referring to Isaiah 53, Peter reminds us that Christ did no wrong (2:22). Jesus truly suffered for doing good. The hands that were nailed to the cross were hands that had healed the sick and touched the lepers. Indeed, not only was Jesus innocent, but the cause of his suffering was *our* sin: 'He himself bore our sins in his body on the tree, so that we might die to sins and live for righteousness; by his wounds you have been healed' (2:24). When we endure what we *don't* deserve, we're to remember the One who endured what we *do* deserve. There may often be times when we suffer for doing good. But we're reminded that we all deserve to suffer at the hand of God's judgment for the evil we've done. But we escape that suffering because 'he himself bore our sins in his body on the tree' (2:24). The same idea emerges at the end of the section: 'It is better, if it is God's will, to suffer for doing good than for doing evil. For Christ died for sins once for all, the righteous for the unrighteous, to bring you to God' (1 Peter 3:17–18). We're to suffer for doing good just as Christ, the righteous One, died for us, the unrighteous.

Second, Peter highlights the way that Christ didn't retaliate when he suffered. 'When they hurled their insults at him, he did not retaliate; when he suffered, he made no threats. Instead, he entrusted himself to him who judges justly' (2:23). That is the Christlike response to suffering – to bear it patiently and to continue trusting God (see also 4:16, 19).

John: 'as I have loved you, so you must love one another'

In John's writings the emphasis is slightly different. Discipleship is seen primarily in terms of love expressed through obedience to the commands of the Father and the Son. Discipleship is based on the rule of love (John 13:34; 15:12; 1 John 4:21; 2 John 5). This love is to be modelled upon the love of God and Jesus (John 13:14, 34; 1 John 2:6; 3:16; 4:11, 16). Yet this equals the way of the cross, because for John love is defined by the cross:

> My command is this: Love each other as I have loved you. Greater love has no-one than this, that he lay down his life for his friends.
> (John 15:12–13)

> This is how we know what love is: Jesus Christ laid down his life for us. And we ought to lay down our lives for our brothers. If anyone has material possessions and sees his brother in need but

> has no pity on him, how can the love of God be in him? Dear children, let us not love with words or tongue but with actions and in truth.
> (1 John 3:16–18)

> This is how God showed his love among us: He sent his one and only Son into the world that we might live through him. This is love: not that we loved God, but that he loved us and sent his Son as an atoning sacrifice for our sins. Dear friends, since God so loved us, we also ought to love one another.
> (1 John 4:9–11)

In each case, we're commanded to love one another. And in each case the love to which we're called is defined by the cross. In other words, the cross is often our model even when it is not explicitly mentioned because references to love in the New Testament imply the cross as the standard of that love.

So the way of the cross, and especially the love demonstrated in the cross, is the essential mark of Christian discipleship under the lordship of Christ. This can certainly involve persecution, but its characteristics are broader in scope. It is characterized by sacrifice, submission, self-denial, service and suffering.

An invitation to die

One of the common characteristics of church planting movements, in which the church grows rapidly, is that they face persecution.[14] There may be many reason why this leads to growth, but let me suggest one.

In the West we often take an incremental approach to discipleship. A person is converted and we begin to ratchet up their commitment to Christ. We start them off with prayer and Bible reading. We then encourage them to 'come out' to their friends and share the gospel. Later we might ask them to serve in church. If they prove very keen, we might encourage them to think about cross-cultural missionary service. We don't even ask people to live among the poor, though we're impressed when they do. Martyrdom is a distant prospect. Through a series of steps, we increase what it means for people to follow Jesus.

But in persecuted churches, martyrdom is written into the call to conversion. A decision to become a Christian might well mean persecution, ostracization or imprisonment. To decide for Christ is to decide for death. Now think about how Jesus issued his evangelistic invitation: 'If anyone would come after me, he must deny himself and take up his cross and follow me' (Mark 8:34). It was an invitation to die.

When the decision for Christ means a decision for martyrdom, everything else is effectively decided. A thousand decisions about money, service, career, lifestyle, reputation are all already made in that one decision to follow Jesus to the end. The choice for martyrdom contains within it a whole life of cross-centred discipleship. And this is the point: not that we should look to be martyred, but that we should call people to cross-shaped lives of self-denial.

When the decision for Christ means a decision for martyrdom, everything else is effectively decided.

Why is the church in the West not growing rapidly? Perhaps one reason is that we haven't made that decision to die. For it's in dying, whether dying as a martyr or dying to self, that we show the worth of Christ to a watching world. He matters more.

A friend of mine was talking about a missionary to the Middle East – let's call him Omar – who converted to

Christianity from a Muslim background. My friend told another convert from Islam that he thought Omar's wife worried too much about money, while Omar himself worried too little. The convert from Islam replied: 'When Omar became a Christian, he gave up everything. He gave up family, reputation and every prospect of wealth. So of course he doesn't worry about money.'

The German theologian Dietrich Bonhoeffer was martyred by the Nazis. One of the least significant of his many honours is that our cat is named after him. In his famous book, *The Cost of Discipleship*, he wrote:

> Thus it begins; the cross is not the terrible end to an otherwise god-fearing and happy life, but it meets us at the beginning of our communion with Christ. When Christ calls a man, he bids him come and die . . . Every command of Jesus is a call to die, with all our affections and lusts . . . The call to discipleship, the baptism in the name of Jesus Christ means both death and life . . . Suffering, then, is the badge of true discipleship . . . This is why Luther reckoned suffering among the marks of the true Church . . . If we refuse to take up our cross and submit to suffering and rejection at the hands of men, we forfeit our fellowship with Christ and have ceased to follow him.[15]

6. EVERYDAY MARTYRDOM

Jesus said, 'If anyone would come after me, he must deny himself and take up his cross daily and follow me' (Luke 9:23). Jesus says we're to take up our cross '*daily*'. The way of the cross is a daily activity. Every day.

WOTC

In recent years bracelets with the mnemonic 'WWJD', standing for 'What Would Jesus Do?', have become popular. Helpful, but not quite helpful enough. The cross is our model. The question we should be asking is: What does it mean to follow the way of the cross? Our bracelets should read 'WDIMTFTWOTC'! Or maybe just 'WOTC'.

What does the practice of the cross mean when someone wrongs me?

'Be kind and compassionate to one another, forgiving each other, just as in Christ God forgave you' (Ephesians 4:32).

What does the practice of the cross mean when I'm tired and someone asks for help?
'But even if I am being poured out like a drink offering on the sacrifice and service coming from your faith, I am glad and rejoice with all of you' (Philippians 2:17).

What does the practice of the cross mean when I want to hold back from taking a risk or moving out of my comfort zone?
'Be imitators of God, therefore, as dearly loved children and live a life of love, just as Christ loved us and gave himself up for us as a fragrant offering and sacrifice to God' (Ephesians 5:1–2).

What does the practice of the cross mean when I see an opportunity to impress someone with my Bible knowledge or Christian service?
'Do nothing out of selfish ambition or vain conceit, but in humility consider others better than yourselves . . . Your attitude should be the same as that of Christ Jesus: Who, being in very nature God, did not consider equality with God something to be grasped, but made himself nothing, taking the very nature of a servant, being made in human likeness. And being found in appearance as a man, he humbled himself and became obedient to death – even death on a cross!' (Philippians 2:3, 5–8).

What does the practice of the cross mean when I start asking, 'How will this affect me?'
'Each of you should look not only to your own interests, but also to the interests of others. Your attitude should be the same as that of Christ Jesus . . . he humbled himself and became obedient to death – even death on a cross!' (Philippians 2:4–5, 8).

What does the practice of the cross mean when my family asks why I've not pursued a career like other people?
'May I never boast except in the cross of our Lord Jesus

Christ, through which the world has been crucified to me, and I to the world' (Galatians 6:14).

What does the practice of the cross mean when people don't respond to my hard work on their behalf?

'To the elders among you, I appeal as a fellow-elder, a witness of Christ's sufferings and one who also will share in the glory to be revealed: Be shepherds of God's flock that is under your care, serving as overseers – not because you must, but because you are willing, as God wants you to be; not greedy for money, but eager to serve' (1 Peter 5:1–2).

What does the practice of the cross mean when I open my wallet?

'See that you also excel in this grace of giving . . . For you know the grace of our Lord Jesus Christ, that though he was rich, yet for your sakes he became poor, so that you through his poverty might become rich' (2 Corinthians 8:7, 9).

What does the practice of the cross mean when I start to say, 'I want my way'?

'Then [Jesus] said to them, "My soul is overwhelmed with sorrow to the point of death. Stay here and keep watch with me." Going a little farther, he fell with his face to the ground and prayed, "My Father, if it is possible, may this cup be taken from me. Yet not as I will, but as you will"' (Matthew 26:38–39).

What does the practice of the cross mean when friends urge me to join them in sinful behaviour?

'Therefore, since Christ suffered in his body, arm yourselves also with the same attitude, because he who has suffered in his body is done with sin . . . They think it strange that you do not plunge with them into the same flood of dissipation, and they heap abuse on you . . .' (1 Peter 4:1, 4).

What does the practice of the cross mean when you receive threatening phone calls?

'Dear friends, do not be surprised at the painful trial you are suffering, as though something strange were happening to you. But rejoice that you participate in the sufferings of Christ, so that you may be overjoyed when his glory is revealed. If you are insulted because of the name of Christ, you are blessed, for the Spirit of glory and of God rests on you' (1 Peter 4:12–14).

What does the practice of the cross mean when I find other Christians difficult to get on with?

'Each of us should please his neighbour for his good, to build him up. For even Christ did not please himself but, as it is written: "The insults of those who insult you have fallen on me" . . . Accept one another, then, just as Christ accepted you, in order to bring praise to God' (Romans 15:2–3, 7).

What does the practice of the cross mean when I get a position of authority?

'Whoever wants to become great among you must be your servant, and whoever wants to be first must be slave of all. For even the Son of Man did not come to be served, but to serve, and to give his life as a ransom for many' (Mark 10:43–45).

What does the practice of the cross mean when I see other Christians in need?

'This is how we know what love is: Jesus Christ laid down his life for us. And we ought to lay down our lives for our brothers. If anyone has material possessions and sees his brother in need but has no pity on him, how can the love of God be in him?' (1 John 3:16–17).

What does the practice of the cross mean when the washing-up needs doing at home?

'Husbands, love your wives, just as Christ loved the church and gave himself up for her' (Ephesians 5:25; see also 1 Peter 2:18 – 3:7).

What does the practice of the cross mean when friends sneer at my faith?
'If you suffer for doing good and you endure it, this is commendable before God. To this you were called, because Christ suffered for you, leaving you an example, that you should follow in his steps. "He committed no sin, and no deceit was found in his mouth." When they hurled their insults at him, he did not retaliate; when he suffered, he made no threats. Instead, he entrusted himself to him who judges justly (1 Peter 2:20–23).

What does the practice of the cross mean when I face temptation?
'Therefore, since Christ suffered in his body, arm yourselves also with the same attitude, because he who has suffered in his body is done with sin. As a result, he does not live the rest of his earthly life for evil human desires, but rather for the will of God' (1 Peter 4:1–2).

Everyday martyrdom

The point is not to learn the list, but to learn the habit, the reflex, the principle. The five Ss of sacrifice, submission, self-denial, service and suffering can be applied in *every* situation.

The way of the cross impacts on both our big life-choices and our small daily actions. It really does include both martyrdom and washing-up. Some of us think we might do well in the big things – at least in theory. But we don't do so well in the small things.

I remember a missionary visiting us, someone who'd moved across continents. That's a big choice to make for you and your family. But he never did the small things. He never offered to help with washing-up, never cleared the table. It made me wonder whether he'd crossed continents because he treasured Christ or because he treasured his reputation.

Every small act of service is a preparation for martyrdom. Indeed, every small act of service is a kind of martyrdom already – a dying to self.

Every small act of service is a preparation for martyrdom. Indeed, every small act of service is a kind of martyrdom already – a dying to self.

Think back to your baptism. What happened? The Bible says a death took place. And a burial. 'Don't you know that all of us who were baptised into Christ Jesus were baptised into his death? We were therefore buried with him through baptism into death in order that, just as Christ was raised from the dead through the glory of the Father, we too may live a new life' (Romans 6:3–4). Baptism shows us that in being united with Christ we've died, died to sin and self. 'For we know that our old self was crucified with him so that the body of sin might be done away with, that we should no longer be slaves to sin' (6). Going under the water, in whatever form that takes, is a picture of our old, dead self being buried. Then we rise to a new life – a life lived for God. 'For Paul, to be in Christ is to be a living exegesis of this narrative of Christ, a new performance of the original drama of exaltation following humiliation, of humiliation as the voluntary renunciation of rights and selfish gain in order to serve and obey.'[16] 'For all of you who were baptised into Christ have clothed yourselves with Christ' (Galatians 3:27), We've put on the costume, we might say. Now we must play the part.

Paul says: 'May I never boast except in the cross of our Lord Jesus Christ, through which the world has been crucified to me, and I to the world' (Galatians 6:14). We've died to the world. To peer pressure. To social constraint. To cultural fads. To the opinion of others. We've identified with the crucified One. Crucifixion was the ultimate symbol of shame in Roman society. The ultimate exclusion. And in Jewish culture it was a curse. The first-century Jewish historian, Josephus, describes it as 'the most miserable of deaths', 'the worst extreme of the tortures inflicted upon slaves', an 'accursed thing', a 'plague'.[17] To take up your cross is to forsake social respectability. To take up your cross is to place yourself outside society and beyond its power.

We're to live as if we're dead. For we are. We've died to our former way of life, to our former selves, to our sinful desires. We've died to the world and its social pressures. Many of us struggle because we're trying to live like spiritual zombies. We're the undead, trying to live the old life that was crucified with Christ. We ask, 'Can I do this?', 'Is this permissible?', 'Is there someone else who could do this?' We want to know what we can get away with, when we should be asking, 'How can I serve Jesus?', 'How can I serve others?'

Michael Jensen was a school chaplain in Australia. He told me how he would tell the pupils one of his favourite stories – the story of Polycarp who was bravely martyred in the second century. When a Roman officer called on him to renounce Christ, Polycarp declared: 'Eighty and six years have I served him and he has done me no wrong. Can I revile my King that saved me?' The officer threatened to have him burned, to which Polycarp replied: 'You try to frighten me with fire that burns for an hour and you forget the fire of hell that never goes out.' To Jensen it was an inspiring story of courage. But he was shocked to discover that the children thought Polycarp was an idiot. 'You've only got one life,' they said. 'You should hold on to it – it's precious.' This experience led Jensen to undertake a PhD on martyrdom. 'Martyrdom,' he says, 'is the external representation of the inner reality of the Christian life.' We witness to another, bigger, fuller life. Martyrdom reveals our hope and the supreme lordship of Jesus in our lives. Renouncing pleasure and security are deeply *impious* acts in a culture which worships the self. They're sacrilegious acts. 'Martyrdom is a sign,' he argues, 'that the Christian way of being a self is completely at odds with the secular way of being a self – and stands as a challenge to it.' Every Christian's life is potentially a martyr's life. But more than that, every Christian's life already *is* a martyr's life. All acts of dying to self are, in a sense, preliminary acts to martyrdom.

Excuses, excuses

Think for a moment about the kind of excuses we make for not putting others before ourselves. 'I've got too much on my plate', 'I'm too busy', 'It's not my job', 'I've got better things to do', 'Other people can do it', 'They'll just let me down. Again.'

> It was just before the Passover Feast. Jesus knew that the time had come for him to leave this world and go to the Father. Having loved his own who were in the world, he now showed them the full extent of his love.
>
> The evening meal was being served, and the devil had already prompted Judas Iscariot, son of Simon, to betray Jesus. Jesus knew that the Father had put all things under his power, and that he had come from God and was returning to God; so he got up from the meal, took off his outer clothing, and wrapped a towel round his waist. After that, he poured water into a basin and began to wash his disciples' feet, drying them with the towel that was wrapped round him.
>
> He came to Simon Peter, who said to him, 'Lord, are you going to wash my feet?'
>
> Jesus replied, 'You do not realise now what I am doing, but later you will understand.'

> 'No,' said Peter, 'you shall never wash my feet.'
>
> Jesus answered, 'Unless I wash you, you have no part with me.'
>
> 'Then, Lord,' Simon Peter replied, 'not just my feet but my hands and my head as well!'
>
> Jesus answered, 'A person who has had a bath needs only to wash his feet; his whole body is clean. And you are clean, though not every one of you.' For he knew who was going to betray him, and that was why he said not every one was clean.
>
> (John 13:1–11)

John says that Jesus 'knew' three things when he washed the disciples' feet. They blow apart our typical excuses for not denying ourselves and serving others.

1. *I've got too much on my plate*

Jesus knows his time has come (1). He knows the cross awaits him. He knows tonight is the night. A short while later, he will be lying on the ground of Gethsemane, sweating drops of blood, sorrowful to the point of death as he contemplates what awaits him. If anyone could have said he was too busy or that he had too much on his mind, it was Jesus.

Yet, asked to perform a small act of service, I say: 'I've got too much on my plate.'

Think about the cross itself:

- Hanging on the cross, in agony and torment, Jesus is thinking of his mother. 'When Jesus saw his mother there, and the disciple whom he loved standing near by, he said to his mother, "Dear woman, here is your son," and to the disciple, "Here is your mother." From that time on, this disciple took her into his home' (John 19:26–27).

- Hanging on the cross, Jesus is thinking of the men condemned with him. 'Then he said, "Jesus, remember me when you come into your kingdom." Jesus answered him, "I tell you the truth, today you will be with me in paradise"' (Luke 23:42–43).
- Hanging on the cross, Jesus is even thinking of his executioners. 'Jesus said, "Father, forgive them, for they do not know what they are doing"' (Luke 23:34).

2. I've got better things to do

We don't often say, 'I'm too important.' That might give away our pomposity. What we say is, 'I've got better things to do. Someone else can do that.'

Jesus knew, John tells us, that he had all authority: 'Jesus knew that the Father had put all things under his power, and that he had come from God and was returning to God' (John 13:3). If anyone could have said he was too important, it was Jesus. After all, he's the One who sustains the universe by his powerful word (Hebrews 1:3). But now he kneels and washes feet.

Yet, asked to perform a small act of service, I say: 'I've got better things to do.'

Again, think about the cross itself: 'Your attitude should be the same as that of Christ Jesus: Who, being in very nature God, did not consider equality with God something to be grasped, but made himself nothing, taking the very nature of a servant, being made in human likeness. And being found in appearance as a man, he humbled himself and became obedient to death – even death on a cross!' (Philippians 2:5–8).

3. They always let me down

'He knew who was going to betray him' (11). Jesus knew Judas had switched sides, become an enemy, become the betrayer. He knew the kiss was coming.

It wasn't as if the rest were much better. They'd spent the last three years misunderstanding him, arguing among themselves, jockeying for position. Soon they would declare their undying loyalty to him, but then to a man forsake him. If anyone could have said 'I don't deserve it', it was Jesus.

Yet, asked to perform a small act of service, I say: 'They always let me down.'

Again think about the cross itself. On the cross Christ dies for his enemies. 'Once you were alienated from God and were enemies in your minds because of your evil behaviour. But now he has reconciled you by Christ's physical body through death to present you holy in his sight, without blemish and free from accusation' (Colossians 1:21–22; see also Romans 5:10).

How, then, does Jesus himself apply his washing of the disciples' feet?

> When he had finished washing their feet, he put on his clothes and returned to his place. 'Do you understand what I have done for you?' he asked them. 'You call me "Teacher" and "Lord", and rightly so, for that is what I am. Now that I, your Lord and Teacher, have washed your feet, you also should wash one another's feet. I have set you an example that you should do as I have done for you. I tell you the truth, no servant is greater than his master, nor is a messenger greater than the one who sent him. Now that you know these things, you will be blessed if you do them.'
> (John 13:12–17)

What will it mean for you to follow the way of the cross in the next five minutes?

What about the next five hours? Or the next five days? In the next five months? Or the next five years?

7. THE VALUE OF JESUS

Jesus once said the kingdom of God was a bit like this.

A man was walking home from working in the fields when he decided to take a short-cut across a scrubby area that never seemed to be used for anything. There was no clear path so he picked his way as best he could. He stumbled a couple of times before tripping over completely, landing in the long grass where he lay dazed. 'And now this,' he thought, recalling yet another hard day in another hard week. Then, a few inches from his head, he noticed a piece of metal sticking out of the ground. Curious, he pulled away the grass and brushed off the topsoil. It was the metal corner of a wooden chest. He tugged away at the tufts of grass and dug at the soil. He pulled and twisted until the chest was free. He paused, and then he lifted the lid. Inside were jewels, pendants, gold coins – all covered in dust, but extremely valuable.

What was he to do? He sat in the sun for a few minutes.

Then he closed the chest, reburied it, kicked soil over it and replaced the tufts of grass as best he could.

That evening he made enquiries. He tracked down the owner of the field and agreed a price. There was some negotiation, a bit of bargaining. He haggled as best he could. But still it was a lot of money. He looked at his savings. Not enough. He asked his relations for a loan. No can do. There was nothing for it. The next day he laid out all his possessions in front of his house – clothes, furniture, utensils, everything. All for sale. House included.

Everyone was curious. What was he doing? Why? Gradually people starting buying. No doubt some great misfortune had befallen him. There were whispered rumours of debts. Most were inclined to pity him. Except that he was smiling broadly. As each item was sold, he would laugh to himself. He seemed hardly able to contain his excitement.

Still, a bargain is a bargain and so people bought his possessions. By mid-morning everyone was keen to get in on the act. Around noon a relative bought his house at a knock-down price. News started to get around and by afternoon neighbouring villagers were buying up his last few possessions. When darkness fell, everything was gone. The man took the money and bought the field.

That night, sleeping under the stars with nothing to his name except one field, he was the happiest man alive. In the morning a new life would begin: a life of prosperity and security, of laughter and hope.

'The kingdom of heaven is like treasure hidden in a field. When a man found it, he hid it again, and then in his joy went and sold all he had and bought that field' (Matthew 13:44).

When Christ is your treasure

In Christ we have a treasure that's worth selling everything to own. Christ is of infinite value. Compared to him, everything else is worthless. To gain Christ, it's worth losing everything.

Not only that. But when we grasp this, when we see the value of Christ, when we see our wonderful inheritance, when he's our treasure, then we'll give up everything *with joy*. 'The kingdom of heaven is like treasure hidden in a field. When a man found it, he hid it again, and then *in his joy* went and sold all he had and bought that field.'

When Christ is your life

When Paul writes to the church in Philippi, he's writing from prison. He's chained up. Plus some Christians are trying to make life difficult for him. You'd think he'd be miserable. Think about what makes you miserable. Paul's there, and yet he's full of joy. He's full of joy because the good news of Jesus is spreading. He's full of joy because he treasures Christ.

> Yes, and I will rejoice, for I know that through your prayers and the help of the Spirit of Jesus Christ this will turn out for my deliverance, as it is my eager expectation and hope that I will not be at all ashamed, but that with full courage now as always Christ will be honoured in my body, whether by life or by death. For to me to live is Christ, and to die is gain. If I am to live in the flesh, that means fruitful labour for me. Yet which I shall choose I cannot tell. I am hard pressed between the two. My desire is to depart and be with Christ, for that is far better. But to remain in the flesh is more necessary on your account. Convinced of this, I know that I will remain and continue with you all, for your progress and joy in the faith, so that in me you may have ample cause to glory in Christ Jesus, because of my coming to you again. (Philippians 1:18–26 ESV)

Paul is confident that he'll be delivered. We might suppose that deliverance for Paul means getting out of prison or at least escaping from martyrdom. But that's not what Paul has in mind because he goes on to debate whether or not he'll die (22–26). He's confident that he'll be delivered, yet he might be martyred!

That's because deliverance for Paul means deliverance from fear and shame and compromise. 'This will turn out for my deliverance, as it is my eager expectation and hope that I will not be at all ashamed, but that with full courage now as always Christ will be honoured in my body, whether by life or by death' (19–20; see also Romans 14:7–9). Maybe he'll honour Christ by living as a faithful servant; maybe he'll honour Christ by dying as a faithful martyr. It doesn't matter which. What matters is that he honours Christ – that he expresses the worth of Christ in the way he lives.

How can Paul talk like this and live like this? The answer is: 'For to me to live is Christ.' When Christ is your life, your treasure, your everything, then death is gain. Death strips you of everything – except Christ. Possessions, position, relationships are all taken away by death. If that's what you live for, then death will be a tragedy. You'll fear and hate and avoid it at all costs. But if you live for Christ, then death is gain. It's gain because you depart to be with Christ – your treasure, your life, your all (23).

This is challenging stuff! But God isn't saying, 'Live a hard life and give up everything.' Paul goes on: 'Convinced of this, I know that I will remain and continue with you all, for your progress and *joy* in the faith, so that in me you may have ample cause to *glory* in Christ Jesus, because of my coming to you again.' What is Paul's hope for Christians? What is the goal of his ministry? It's that they might have *joy*. He wants us to *glory* in Christ Jesus. He's offering treasure – a treasure worth giving up everything to possess – the treasure of knowing and serving Jesus Christ. The call isn't to a hard life; it is to find joy in Christ – and then live accordingly.

This is how Paul puts it in chapter 3: 'I count everything as loss because of the surpassing worth of knowing Christ Jesus my Lord. For his sake I have suffered the loss of all things and count them as rubbish, in order that I may gain Christ' (3:8 ESV). That sums it up. That's Paul's story. It's the story of the man with the field. Paul is that man. 'I found this treasure – the all-surpassing treasure of knowing Christ Jesus my Lord. And in my joy, I sold everything to own this treasure. I count everything loss and rubbish so that I may gain Christ.'

You reveal the value you put on Christ, argues John Piper, by what you are willing to risk or give up for him.[18] The way we use our money and time demonstrates, without fail, the value we put on Christ. Any money you have has been given by God so that you might use it to show that Christ, not money, is your treasure. It's the same with houses, cars, career, friends, reputation, abilities and suffering. If you truly know the glory of Christ, then you'll value him even above life itself. Elsewhere Paul says: 'I only know that in every city the Holy Spirit warns me that prison and hardships are facing me. However, I consider my life worth nothing to me, if only I may finish the race and complete the task the Lord Jesus has given me – the task of testifying to the gospel of God's grace' (Acts 20:23–24).

What difference will treasuring Christ make:

- When you're feeling miserable?
- When you envy other people?
- When going to the prayer meeting feels like a struggle?
- When you start to complain?

The eighteenth-century preacher Richard Burnham was briefly a pastor in Staines (where I used to be a pastor), after which he led a congregation in the City of London. It was said of him that he 'sought his happiness in all kinds of worldly amusements before being brought under serious impressions through Wesleyan preachers'. He wrote one of my favourite hymns, a hymn that expresses the worth of knowing Christ crucified:

> To know my Jesus crucified,
> by far excels all things beside;
> all earthly goods we count but loss
> and triumph in our Saviour's cross.
>
> Knowledge of all terrestrial things
> never our souls true pleasure brings;
> no peace, but in the Son of God;
> no joy, but through his pardoning blood.
>
> O could we know and love him more
> and all his wondrous grace explore,
> we would not envy man's esteem,
> but part with all and follow him.
>
> Lord, may we bear our every loss;
> be patient under every cross;
> never may we our Saviour blame,
> though we're despised for his dear name.
>
> Thus make us willing, glorious Lamb,
> to suffer all things for your name;
> at last be where our Jesus is
> and rise to everlasting bliss.

We should avoid, not a *wounded* life, says John Piper, but a *wasted* life. 'Some of you will die in the service of Christ. That will not be a tragedy. Treasuring life above Christ is a tragedy.'[19] Imagine reaching the end of your life and realizing you had wasted it. Piper illustrates with two stories:

> In April 2000, Ruby Eliason and Laura Edwards were killed in Cameroon, West Africa. Ruby was over eighty. Single all her life, she poured it out for one great thing: to make Jesus Christ known among the unreached, the poor, and the sick. Laura was a widow, a medical doctor, pushing eighty years old, and serving at Ruby's side in Cameroon. The brakes failed, the car went over a cliff, and they were both killed instantly. I asked my congregation: Was that a tragedy? Two lives, driven by one great passion, namely, to be spent in unheralded service to the perishing poor for the glory of Jesus Christ – even two decades after most of their American counterparts had retired to throw away their lives on trifles. No, that is not a tragedy. That is a glory. These lives were not wasted. And these lives were not lost. 'Whoever loses his life for my sake and the gospel's will save it' (Mark 8:35).
>
> I will tell you what a tragedy is. I will show you how to waste your life. Consider a story from the February 1998 edition of *Reader's Digest*, which tells about a couple who 'took early retirement from their jobs in the Northeast five years ago when he was 59 and she was 51. Now they live in Punta Gorda, Florida, where they cruise on their 30 foot trawler, play softball and collect shells.' At first, when I read it, I thought it might be a joke. A spoof on the American Dream. But it wasn't. Tragically, this was the dream: Come to the end of your life – your one and only precious, God-given life – and let the last great work of your life, before you give an account to your Creator, be this: playing softball and collecting shells. Picture them before Christ at the great day of judgment: 'Look, Lord. See my shells.' *That*

> is a tragedy. And people today are spending billions of dollars to persuade you to embrace that tragic dream. Over against that, I put my protest: Don't buy it. Don't waste your life.[20]

I believe you'll actually discover more of the worth of Christ and the joy of serving him, the more you risk for him and the more you give for him. Too often, we can't quite lay hold of the treasure of Christ with both hands because we're still clinging to the baubles of this world.

Too often, we can't quite lay hold of the treasure of Christ with both hands because we're still clinging to the baubles of this world.

Let go of whatever is in your hand and take hold of the glory of Christ. Piper again:

> What a tragic waste when people turn away from the Calvary road of love and suffering. All the riches of the glory of God in Christ are on that road. All the sweetest fellowship with Jesus is there. All the treasures of assurance. All the ecstasies of joy. All the clearest sightings of eternity. All the noblest camaraderie. All the humblest affections. All the most tender acts of forgiving kindness. All the deepest discoveries of God's Word. All the most earnest prayers. They are all on the Calvary road where Jesus walks with his people. Take up your cross and follow Jesus. On this road, and this road alone, life is Christ and death is gain. Life on every other road is wasted.[21]

Here are the words of Rashid, a Pakistani who, when he became a Christian, was rejected by his family, and whose wife was forced to leave him, taking his daughter.

> Some might conclude that my life is pitiable. After all, every evening after I finish my shift I go home to an empty flat, one

not filled with the gleeful shouts of a six-year-old child. When I go to bed at night, there is no one beside me to say, 'I love you.' I expect never to hear from my parents on my birthday, or on any other day for that matter. The only noise in my home comes from the television set, and that I do not watch very often.

But to pity me would be to miss the joy I have experienced. I believe things are better now than they were before I was a Christian. My house might be quiet, but I am not lonely. My family may have forsaken me, but I am not abandoned. I have Christ, and that is enough. Indeed, it is more than enough. In my eyes, I have been blessed beyond measure, far greater than I deserve and more than I could have hoped.[22]

8. THE WAY OF THE CROSS = THE WAY OF JOY

I'd been brooding all morning. I'd rehearsed what I would say over and over again. And each time, the justice of my position seemed more and more evident! It was a small thing, I knew, but it was really bugging me, wrecking any sense of inner peace. Why was that? I tried to analyse what was going on in my heart. Was I in the wrong? Right was on my side, I concluded. So why couldn't I let it go? And then it hit me. I was acting as if *I* was what mattered in the world. So what if I'd been mistreated? It wasn't about me. It was about God and his glory. Suddenly any slight done to me seemed small and insignificant. My knotted, brooding heart was set free. I could laugh it off and rejoice in my beautiful God.

The way of the cross is the way of joy

The way of the cross is a tough ask. It's the way of self-denial. It is, says Jesus, like losing yourself. Yet Christians can accept the way of the cross with great joy. We should embrace it, welcome it, delight in it. Is that because we're masochists? Because we feel the need to suffer for our guilt? Are we trying to self-atone? By no means.

We gladly accept the way of the cross because it's the way of joy. After washing the feet of his disciples and commending his humble service as a model for all believers, Jesus says: 'Now that you know these things, you will be blessed if you do them' (John 13:17). This is the way of blessing. And when he first called his disciples to the way of the cross he said:

> If anyone would come after me, he must deny himself and take up his cross and follow me. For whoever wants to save his life will lose it, but whoever loses his life for me and for the gospel will save it. What good is it for a man to gain the whole world, yet forfeit his soul? Or what can a man give in exchange for his soul? If anyone is ashamed of me and my words in this adulterous and sinful generation, the Son of Man will be ashamed of him when he comes in his Father's glory with the holy angels. (Mark 8:34–38)

In losing ourselves, we gain ourselves. In losing life, we gain life. If we share in Christ's suffering, we will also share in his eternal glory. But even in this life, we find ourselves as we deny ourselves.

I was watching football one night on television when I got a phone call. It was Aram, an asylum seeker who for a couple of years had become very much part of our lives. Then he moved to Holland in search of refugee status. From time to time he would phone, usually when he was bored and wanted to kill time. I was annoyed to hear his voice. It meant interrupting my football.

But Aram cut straight to the chase. He'd been reading, in his native language, a Christian book that someone had sent him (my friend Samuel as it turned out) and he couldn't put it down. He was even reluctant to stop in order to eat. He wasn't sure what the book was, but after reading and translating some of the opening lines to me, it became clear it was the New Testament.

Then he asked me if I could interpret dreams. So, with a quick prayer to God, I invited him to tell me his dream. It involved his (deceased) father trying to kill him. It was a recurrent dream that was clearly disturbing him. 'Your dream', I suggested to him, 'represents the opposition you will receive from your family if you become a Christian.' So we read from Matthew 10:26–39 together. I read a verse in English, he read it in his native language, and then he translated it into English. In this passage Jesus says:

> But don't be afraid of those who threaten you. For the time is coming when everything that is covered will be revealed, and all that is secret will be made known to all. What I tell you now in the darkness, shout abroad when daybreak comes. What I whisper in your ear, shout from the housetops for all to hear!
>
> Don't be afraid of those who want to kill your body; they cannot touch your soul. Fear only God, who can destroy both soul and body in hell. What is the price of two sparrows – one copper coin? But not a single sparrow can fall to the ground without your Father knowing it. And the very hairs on your head are all numbered. So don't be afraid; you are more valuable to God than a whole flock of sparrows.
>
> Everyone who acknowledges me publicly here on earth, I will also acknowledge before my Father in heaven. But everyone who denies me here on earth, I will also deny before my Father in heaven.
>
> Don't imagine that I came to bring peace to the earth! I came not to bring peace, but a sword.

> I have come to set a man against his father,
> a daughter against her mother,
> and a daughter-in-law against her mother-in-law.
> Your enemies will be right in your own household!
>
> If you love your father or mother more than you love me, you are not worthy of being mine; or if you love your son or daughter more than me, you are not worthy of being mine. If you refuse to take up your cross and follow me, you are not worthy of being mine. If you cling to your life, you will lose it; but if you give up your life for me, you will find it.
>
> (Matthew 10:26–39 NLT)

Despite its challenging message, Aram found it 'beautiful'. He began translating the final verse and then asked, 'So even if I'm a loser, I'm really a winner?' I was about to say, that's not quite the right translation, when I thought, 'No, that's a pretty good paraphrase.'

Self-fulfilment versus self-denial

The way of the cross is the way of blessing because human beings were made to love God and love others. It's our self-centredness that leads to so many of our emotional problems. We find wholeness in being God-centred rather than self-centred. When I'm grumpy it's because I want this world to be my world. I want events to go my way. Of course things don't go my way and so I feel despondent or bitter. But when I take up my cross, I deny myself, I crucify myself. I say, 'This is God's world, not mine. Things are not under my control, they're under God's control. And he has loved me and died for me.' I say with Jesus: 'Not my will, but yours be done.'

David Wells argues that, by removing God from public life, we've also removed what it means to be truly human.[23] The 'death' of God in our culture has led to the death of the human being. That's because, without God, we're left with no basis for moral judgments. Judgments can only be reflections of our own feelings. This in turn has shifted us from talking about 'character' to talking about 'personality'. The old moral concern with personal restraint and sacrifice has given way to a new concern for self-realization and self-expression. Everyone 'must' be themselves, express themselves, realize themselves. We must be self-made people, buying whatever we need to this end. Self-denial is no longer a virtue, but a sin against the self. It's seen as dangerously repressive, threatening a person's self-realization. What should the man who's tempted to have an affair do? We used to say he should deny himself for the sake of his marriage and family. Now our culture says his first duty is to find himself by expressing his desires. What should the woman who feels worthless do? We used to say she would find her worth in serving others. Now our culture encourages her to buy new clothes to make her feel good about herself – even if that means racking up credit card debt. What should someone do when looking for employment? We used to value serving the community, but now our culture encourages us to find self-fulfilment through our work. And so it goes on.

We can easily do a 'Christian' version of this in which Christianity becomes a means of self-realization. My personal growth or experience is what counts. My first responsibility is to myself – to develop my spiritual side – not to serve others in humility. People are encouraged to identify their spiritual gifts and serve through activities they find fulfilling. In fact, in the New Testament, Christians are never encouraged to identify their gifts. The teaching on gifts is always addressed to the community as a whole, to encourage us to celebrate the differences among us. Christians are instead encouraged to deny themselves and serve others. David Henderson comments:

> Because God no longer occupies centre stage, terms like self-love, self-expression, self-confidence, and self-fulfilment, none of which graces the pages of the Scriptures, begin to dominate the church's conversation. Meanwhile other 'self' words straight from the Bible like self-surrender, self-sacrifice, self-denial, and self-control slip into disuse . . . When this happens, we may be preaching, we may be sharing faith, but what we are communicating is not genuine Christianity. In Christianity, the one place the self cannot be is at the centre. That is the rightful place of God alone.[24]

Has our culture's obsession with self made us any happier? Of course not. We're wired by God to love him and love others: to find ourselves in losing ourselves. Meic Pearse, Professor of History at Houghton College, New York, writes:

> The possession of things is what gives us a self-made identity ('I'm a Goth'; 'I'm a bookish person'; 'I'm a sophisticate – just look at my clothes!') . . . But, since such identities are so clearly malleable and vulnerable to the ravages of age, the vagaries of relative economic status, and the whims of fashion, we are left vulnerable . . . We want a stable family, of course . . . but not if it stands in the way of my right to do what I want . . . We value community, we say . . . but the last thing we want is to be required to live in one place, alongside the same people, for the course of our entire lives. In other words, we really and truly want none of these things . . . But if there's one thing all that psychology could have taught us, it's that the self-directed person remains, in most respects, an infant. Growing up consists in becoming other-centred. That is why Jesus was the most grown-up person who ever lived.[25]

Our self-love makes our relationships brittle. Cross-centred love, in contrast, is 'in it for the long haul'. Such love 'is not surprised by difficulty or even rejection but finds joy in the challenge of lasting through difficult circumstances'.[26]

In the face of these deep cultural shifts, we need to say: a life of self-denial really is the good life. You really will experience more of God washing dishes than meditating on retreat. The thought-provoking film, *Bruce Almighty*, gets a lot wrong about God, but this it gets right: if you want to draw near to God, then clean floors with him.

Living in a small, lonely kingdom

If our lives are focused on ourselves rather than God, if we're not denying ourselves, then our lives will shrink to the size of our petty concerns. We will become self-obsessed, living with small horizons.

If you're anxious about how others perceive you, if you're angry when others slight you, if you're focused on a pay rise or a new gadget, then you live in a very small world – a world that can never satisfy. You were made for something much bigger. 'When God enters our lives by his grace, he isn't working to make our kingdom work so much as he is calling us to an excitement with, and dedication to, a much greater kingdom.'[27] When we choose to be god of our own lives, we choose a small kingdom of one, lonely person. The person who gets angry in the supermarket queue is a small person living in a small world.

I've made getting off a train an art form. I leave my seat shortly before the train arrives in the station, then stand in the centre of the aisle until I know on which side of the train the platform will be. I don't want to stand by one door and have the person behind me exit first when the platform appears on the other side. As the train slows down, I need to work out where the exit is, so I can be marching up the platform before other people get into their stride. What's the point?

The point, of course, is to get out of the station ten seconds before anyone else. To be ahead. To be first.

We go through life wanting to be first. To be one step ahead. As children, we fight over toys and argue about the last sweet. As we grow up, we learn to be polite, which just means that our jockeying for position becomes more sophisticated. But still we strive to be the first, the centre, the most, the best. It's hard work. It wears us down. But our very self is at stake. And so we grind on, even as we are ground down. We're all 'glory junkies', explains Paul Tripp. That's why we relish a great goal, a beautiful dress, a dramatic sunset, a delicious cake. We work hard for these moments. But these are 'just the shadow glories of the created world. We were made for the one glory that is transcendent – the glory of God. When you grasp this, your life begins to make a difference.'[28]

Dave's parents were disappointed in their son. He'd turned his back on a career in order to work with refugees. It seemed such a waste. He was approaching thirty with no discernable prospects, no place on the property ladder, no standing in society. As his pastor, I was under suspicion, partly to blame for his reckless choices. That was a few years ago. Today the attitude of Dave's father is totally different. He sees the impact Dave is having, the eternal fruit from his life. He realizes that, were Dave to die, he would leave a big hole in many people's lives. Dave's father has started asking himself what he's done with his own life. He's built up a successful business and made money, but realizes he's leaving no lasting legacy.

The thing is this. The way of the cross is a life of sacrifice. But sometimes, after a while, the sacrifices don't feel like sacrifices. They feel like better options. Consider the couple who move from the leafy suburbs to the inner city. Sacrifice?

The way of the cross is a life of sacrifice. But sometimes, after a while, the sacrifices don't feel like sacrifices. They feel like better options.

Maybe not. Maybe they've realized that the excitement and joy of serving God, of seeing him glorified in the lives of people, of working to plant a church in a difficult area, the eternal 'well done, good and faithful servant' – that these things offer more than the en-suite bathroom and the second car. Sacrifice? I don't think so.

The way of the cross is the way of my Saviour

John Chapman says: 'We often speak about the cross as if there were no-one on it.' The way of the cross is not an abstract standard or code. It's not like tithing where you can give the standard a numerical value.

Our standard is a person. And our standard is not just a good person; not even *the* good person. Our standard is our Saviour. My Saviour. Your Saviour.

The way of the cross is the way of Jesus. All the love I feel for Jesus attaches itself to the way of the cross. All the beauty I see in Jesus attaches itself to the way of the cross. Why do I want to follow this hard road? Because it represents all that makes my Saviour attractive. I want to be like him. Of course I do. He's so wonderful, so beautiful, so lovely. And to be like him means above all else to walk the way of the cross. 'To deny oneself is to be aware only of Christ and no more of self, to see only him who goes before and no more the road which is too hard for us.'[29]

Our standard isn't just love. It's not just some great story of love that we can read about. My standard is the love Jesus showed *to me*. It's the cross on which he died *my* death, bore *my* sin, took *my* punishment. It's *my* cross.

The way of the cross is love responding to love. The love of the cross wins the love of our cold hearts.

When I survey the wondrous cross
On which the Prince of Glory died,
My richest gain I count but loss,
And pour contempt on all my pride.

Forbid it, Lord, that I should boast,
Save in the death of Christ my God!
All the vain things that charm me most,
I sacrifice them to His blood.

See from His head, His hands, His feet,
Sorrow and love flow mingled down!
Did e'er such love and sorrow meet,
Or thorns compose so rich a crown?

His dying crimson, like a robe,
Spreads o'er His body on the tree;
Then I am dead to all the globe,
And all the globe is dead to me.

Were the whole realm of nature mine,
That were a present far too small;
Love so amazing, so divine,
Demands my soul, my life, my all.
(Isaac Watts, 1674–1748)

Back to the pardon of the cross

The way of the cross will crush you if you don't embrace the pardon of the cross. And that's not just valid for back then, when you first went to God for forgiveness. But day by day by day. Every morning we need to wake up and say, 'There is now no condemnation.' Actually it's easy to do this in the morning. You need to do it in the evening. You need to do it when you sin. When you look with lust. When you lose your temper. When you don't show sacrificial love. You need to say, 'There is now no condemnation.'

Because otherwise the way of the cross will crush you. After all, what a standard it is! The love of Jesus for his enemies!

At one point Jesus sent his disciples out on what proved to be a successful mission. When they returned, they excitedly reported all that had happened. Jesus responded: 'Do not rejoice that the spirits submit to you, but rejoice that your names are written in heaven' (Luke 10:20).

Luke then recounts the famous parable of the good Samaritan (25–37). Jesus is telling the story in response to a question from a teacher of the law. The teacher asks, 'What must I do to inherit eternal life?' He wants to know what he must do to be right with God. Jesus says, in effect, 'It's very simple. Love God. Love your neighbour.' It's not complicated. Now, a moment's thought and I know I'm stuffed, because I haven't loved God and I haven't loved by neighbour. But the lawyer keeps going. He wants to pin it down. Luke says: 'He wanted to justify himself, so he asked Jesus, "And who is my neighbour?"' (29).

He wants to be able to tick off 'Love for neighbour'. Done. Justified. So he needs to know who his neighbour is. Is it my family or my village? Jesus, of course, tells the story of the good Samaritan. His neighbour is anyone in need – even if that person is an enemy.

If you're trying to justify yourself, to prove yourself, to establish your identity, then this blows your plans apart. You can't do it. If your joy and identity are found in ministry, then ministry will crush you.

But if you live within the grace of God, with confidence that there is now no condemnation, then you can embrace this as the good life. This is the way of your Saviour.

Don't think of this lawyer as some legalistic nutcase. The lawyer is you and I. Deep down we want to make it on our own, or at least contribute to the process. We want to prove ourselves. We want to impress. We want to establish our identity. We want to feel good about what we've done. We want others to like or respect us. So we ask, 'What do I need to do? What are my responsibilities? What are your expectations? What do I need to do in this church to be accepted? What do I need to do in mission to be approved? Do I need to come to this meeting? If I do these activities, will that mean I'm okay?'

But I don't want you ticking off some list. I want your love. I'm jealous for God and I want you to love God and love your neighbour.

And you will not love God if you're trying to prove or justify yourself. You'll think of God as a judge or a boss or a superintendent: scoring you, marking you, checking the tick boxes. And all the time, God is saying, 'You can't justify yourself. You don't need to justify yourself. Rejoice that your names are written in heaven. Jesus has done it all. All I want is your love.' So start each day with a prayer along the following lines: 'Loving Father, I thank you that there is now no condemnation for those who are in Christ Jesus. Please show me how I can love you today and how I can love my neighbour.'

Don't move on to the next chapter just yet. Put the book down and find someone to serve. Step out on the path of blessing (John 13:17 NLT).

Part Three:
The pattern of the cross and resurrection – suffering followed by glory

The resurrection of Jesus is the promise and beginning of God's new world. But the shadow of the cross still hangs over history, revealing the reality of human sin and God's judgment. The kingdom of God is a hidden kingdom until Jesus Christ is revealed in glory. So the pattern for Christians is one of suffering now, followed by glory.

9. NO GLORY WITHOUT THE CROSS

No glory without the cross #1 (Mark 8)

> Some people brought a blind man and begged Jesus to touch him. [Jesus] took the blind man by the hand and led him outside the village. When he had spat on the man's eyes and put his hands on him, Jesus asked, 'Do you see anything?'
>
> [The man] looked up and said, 'I see people; they look like trees walking around.'
>
> Once more Jesus put his hands on the man's eyes. Then his eyes were opened, his sight was restored, and he saw everything clearly.

That's the story Mark tells at a pivotal point in his Gospel (8:22–25). It has a number of similarities to another story a few verses earlier in which Jesus opens the ears of a deaf man. The stories form a pair. In both Jesus takes the man aside from the crowd (7:33; 8:23) and in both Jesus spits (7:33; 8:23).

In both there's an emphasis upon speaking plainly or seeing clearly: 'At this, the man's ears were opened, his tongue was loosened and he began to speak plainly' (7:35). 'Then his eyes were opened, his sight was restored, and he saw everything clearly' (8:25).

These stories are about eyes and ears being opened, about hearing properly and seeing clearly. In between, we discover the disciples struggling to *see* who Jesus is and to *hear* his words with understanding. They don't yet recognize Jesus as God's promised King. Jesus has already fed 5,000 people. Now he does it all over again with 4,000 people (6:30–44; 8:1–9). But still they don't get it. They're like the deaf man and the blind man. 'Do you have eyes but fail to see, and ears but fail to hear? And don't you remember?' Jesus says to them. 'Do you still not understand?' (Mark 8:18, 21).

And then the tension is finally broken. At last the disciples recognize Jesus as the Messiah. In Matthew's account Jesus tells Peter, 'This was . . . revealed to you . . . by my Father in heaven'. Mark makes the same point by squeezing the healing of the blind man in between the 'Do you still not understand?' of 8:21 and Peter's confession that Jesus is the Messiah in 8:29. In between unbelief and belief is the story of a blind man enabled to see by a miracle. Jesus says, 'Do you still not see or understand? . . . Do you have eyes but fail to see?' And then he heals a blind man. And then the disciples see who Jesus is.

The implication is clear: the disciples understand who Jesus is, just as the deaf man hears and the blind man sees. Recognizing Jesus as the King requires a miracle. Faith is a work of God's grace. This gives us humility and confidence. Our faith in Jesus is an act of grace, not the product of human achievement. And we can't make people Christians or give them faith – that's God's job. Our job is to proclaim the gospel and leave God to open blind eyes and deaf ears. 'He has done everything well . . . He even makes the deaf hear and the mute speak' (7:37).

But we're only halfway there. Have you ever wondered why it takes two attempts for Jesus to heal the blind man? Jesus puts his hands on the man's eyes and the man half sees. He sees people who look like trees. Jesus puts his hands on the man a second time, and this time he sees clearly. Did Jesus get it wrong first time round, like a half-baked spell that turns the frog into a prince but with a frog's head?

The answer is that this healing illustrates the process by which the disciples come to faith in Jesus the King. The miracle is in two stages because the disciples are only halfway there. They see that Jesus is the King. Now they must see that he's the King who must suffer and die. He's the King who rules through sacrificial love.

'He then began to teach them that the Son of Man must suffer . . .' (8:31). The 'then' is significant: now that they've recognized him as the Messiah, Jesus can began to tell them what it really means for him to be the Messiah. Now that they've learnt lesson one, he can start teaching lesson two. We're told, 'He spoke plainly about this . . .' (8:32). The disciples assume that messiahship means exercising power and glory. Jesus needs to reprogramme their thinking: 'The Son of Man must suffer . . .'

As Jesus was speaking plainly about his sufferings, 'Peter took him aside and began to rebuke him. But when Jesus turned and looked at his disciples, he rebuked Peter. "Get behind me, Satan!" he said. "You do not have in mind the things of God, but the things of men"' (8:32–33). A few minutes before – quite literally – Peter had made a great, climactic statement of faith. Now he's doing Satan's work. What a turnaround. And it's because he only partially sees who

Jesus is. He's like the blind man seeing people like trees. Peter sees that Jesus is the King, but he can't see that Jesus is the King who must suffer and die. Recognizing Jesus as the Messiah is only halfway to recognizing the true nature of his identity and mission. Jesus' words, 'Get behind me, Satan!' echo his words, 'Away from me, Satan!' to Satan himself in the wilderness. There Satan had offered him the kingdom without the cross (Matthew 4:8–10). Again Satan makes that offer, this time through Peter. Again, Jesus rejects glory without the cross.

Jesus not only rebukes Peter, but says that his cross will become their cross. Having declared that the cross must be central to his identity and mission, he declares that the cross must be central to their identity and mission. As Dietrich Bonhoeffer says, Jesus 'makes it clear beyond all doubt that the "must" of suffering applies to his disciples no less than to himself. Just as Christ is Christ only in virtue of his suffering and rejection, so the disciple is a disciple only in so far as he shares his lord's suffering and rejection and crucifixion.'[30]

Mark describes his book as 'the gospel about Jesus Christ, the Son of God' (1:1). The first half of Mark's Gospel climaxes in Peter's confession: Jesus is the Christ (8:29). The second half takes place as Jesus travels to, and arrives at, Jerusalem – the place of his crucifixion. The cross dominates the second half of the gospel. And this second half climaxes in another confession, the confession of the centurion, that Jesus is the Son of God. And this confession is made when he 'heard his cry and saw how he died' (15:39).

We look for God in the great acts of creation, in miracles, in displays of power. Jesus does these things: he calms the storm, he casts out evil spirits, he heals the sick and raises the dead. But the fullest revelation of God is not in power and glory, but in the foolishness, shame and weakness of the cross. The cross is how much God loves us. The cross is what he will do to rescue us from our sin. The cross is how he achieves his victory. The cross is how he exercises his reign. The One on the throne of heaven is the Lamb who was slain (Revelation 5:5–6).

No glory without the cross #2 (Mark 9)

The declaration by Jesus that he must suffer and that his disciples must also take up their cross to follow him is succeeded in Mark's Gospel by the story of the transfiguration. Here we see Jesus in his true glory. Here we hear the affirmation of the Father. But what does the voice from heaven say? We might expect it to say, 'This is my Son, whom I love. Gaze upon him. Feast your eyes on his radiant glory.' But that's not what the Father says. He says: 'This is my Son, whom I love. Listen to him!' (9:7). Why does he say 'Listen to him'? Because that was precisely what the disciples had refused to do a few days earlier. When Jesus spoke about the cross, Peter rebuked him, rejecting his words, refusing to listen. In other words, the voice from heaven affirms the way of the cross.

When Peter confessed Jesus as the Christ, 'Jesus warned them not to tell anyone about him' (8:30). Again, as Peter, James and John came down from the mountain where Jesus was transfigured, 'Jesus gave them orders not to tell anyone what they had seen until the Son of Man had risen from the dead' (9:9). Jesus said he'd come to proclaim the good news (1:38). He'd commissioned the disciples to proclaim that message (3:14). So why does he tell them to keep quiet? Why does he command them *not* to tell people about him?

The answer is that Jesus doesn't want his messianic identity revealed until people realize he's the Messiah who must suffer and die. If people think of him simply as a King of glory, then they'll misunderstand him badly. He doesn't want people to follow him if they simply think of him as a King of power. He wants us to follow the servant King. Before we can proclaim the Messiah, we must understand that he's the Messiah who dies.

All evangelism must include the message of the cross and the call to follow the cross. There is, sadly, plenty of preaching today that effectively leaves out the cross. It promises prosperity, health and victory. But it doesn't speak of sin, judgment and the need for the pardoning blood of Christ. It doesn't speak of repentance, sacrifice and suffering. But there can be no true proclamation of Jesus without the cross. We can't speak of his glory without speaking of his cross. Seeing Jesus = seeing the cross. Proclaiming Jesus = proclaiming the cross.

No glory without the cross #3 (Mark 10)

'Teacher,' they said, 'we want you to do for us whatever we ask.' Would you fall for it? Jesus certainly didn't. 'What do you want me to do for you?' he replied. James and John have sidled up to Jesus. They want something. 'Let one of us sit at your right and the other at your left in your glory.' They ask for power and glory. But without the cross. Jesus asks, 'Can you drink the cup I drink or be baptised with the baptism I am baptised with?' (10:35–38). By this he means his sufferings (14:36). He is saying, in effect, 'If you want to share my glory, you'll first need to share my suffering.' The way to glory is the way of the cross.

The other disciples are no better. They're furious when they find out what James and John have been up to (10:41). So Jesus calls them together. 'Whoever wants to become great among you must be your servant,' he tells them, 'and whoever wants to be first must be slave of all. For even the Son of Man did not come to be served, but to serve, and to give his life as a ransom for many' (10:43–45). The way to greatness is the way of the cross.

Mark then tells the story of a blind man called Bartimaeus. When Bartimaeus hears that Jesus is passing, he calls out, 'Jesus, Son of David, have mercy on me!' The crowd try to shut him up, but he persists. Jesus stops and calls him over. And then Jesus asks him a strange question: 'What do you want me to do for you?' (10:51). Surely it's obvious! There's a blind man standing in front of Jesus. He's just been led through the crowds. He wants to see. The point is, though, that this is exactly the same question that Jesus put to James and John in the previous story – word for word. 'What do you want me to do for you?' (10:36). Mark wants us to draw a parallel between these two stories.

The pattern for Jesus is suffering followed by glory. The pattern for his followers is suffering followed by glory. But James and John don't understand this. They don't *see* it. They're blind. Their answer to the question, 'What do you want me to do for you?' should have been the answer that Bartimaeus gave, 'Rabbi, I want to see' (10:51). Jesus needs to open the eyes of Bartimaeus, but he also needs to open the eyes of the disciples. They too need to see: to see that the Messiah must suffer, to see the importance of the way of the cross, to see the pattern of suffering followed by glory.

When Bartimaeus is healed, we're told he 'followed Jesus along the road' (10:52). The road to where? It's the road to Jerusalem and the road to the cross. At the beginning of the story Bartimaeus is 'by the roadside' (10:46), but by the end he is 'on the way' (10:52 ESV; see Acts 9:2; 19:9, 23; 22:4; 24:22). James and John want to take a bypass round the cross and reach their destination – glory – the easy way. That's because they don't see clearly. But Bartimaeus, sight restored, follows Jesus along the road to the cross.

10. BONDAGE FOLLOWED BY LIBERATION – THE PATTERN FOR THE WORLD

An advert for the campaign, *Make Poverty History*. Brad Pitt appears against a white background. Pauses. Then clicks his fingers. He's followed by Davina McCall. *Click*. Colin Firth. *Click*. George Clooney. *Click*. Kate Moss. *Click. Click*. Bono. *Click*. And so on. Liam Neeson provides the voice-over: 'A child dies completely unnecessarily as a result of extreme poverty every three seconds. *Click*. There we go. That's another one. *Click*. Somebody's daughter. *Click*. Somebody's son. And the thing is . . . *Click* . . . all these deaths are avoidable.' On the screen come the words: 'Make Poverty History. You can change the world.'

Can we make poverty history *in* history? Can we change the world?

Television news, October 1998. The newscaster announces the opening of a public enquiry into the deaths of 150 children during operations at the Bristol Royal Infirmary between 1984 and 1995.

> It will cost at least £15 million and could take up to two years, but campaigners already say its scope will be too limited.
>
> Tim Rogers reports:
>
> 'Among the early arrivals at the enquiry this morning, Tracey Clark from Devon is the first of scores of parents who will give evidence about their own personal tragedy. Her eleven-month-old baby Melissa died following a heart operation at the Bristol Royal Infirmary. And her mother, like many other parents, believes that their babies died because of the surgeon's incompetence. It's that central allegation and the implications for the health service that the enquiry will investigate . . .
>
> 'Parents like Trevor James now want a change in the system. He says the circumstances resulting in the death of his baby daughter Bethany should never be repeated.'

Can we prevent children from dying during operations? Can we stop tragedies happening?

The cross reveals human rebellion

The cross is the supreme expression of divine love. Like nothing else, it shows the greatness of God's love. But the cross is also the supreme expression of human sin.

In looking at discipleship as the way of the cross, we've spoken of suffering and service as that which is voluntarily accepted by disciples as they deny themselves and take up their cross. Suffering, however, is not always like this. It's not always, or even commonly, worthy, nor voluntarily accepted. More often, it's inflicted upon the sufferer against his or her will. Yet the basic assertion holds true: present reality bears the mark of the cross. This is so because the cross is at one and the same time both the fullest expression of love and the fullest expression of evil. The cross is an example for us to follow, but it's also more than an example to follow.

It represents the climax of human rebellion against God. In Psalm 2, the psalmist speaks of the raging of the nations against God and against his anointed king.

> Why do the nations conspire
> and the peoples plot in vain?
> The kings of the earth take their stand
> and the rulers gather together
> against the LORD
> and against his Anointed One.
> 'Let us break their chains,' they say,
> 'and throw off their fetters.'
> (Psalm 2:1–3)

The early church recognized that this rebellion had come to its climax in the cross. As the believers in the early church prayed, they quoted these words from Psalm 2 and continued: 'Indeed Herod and Pontius Pilate met together with the Gentiles and the people of Israel in this city to conspire against your holy servant Jesus, whom you anointed' (Acts 4:27). The rejection of God which is characteristic of humanity in every age has reached its apotheosis in the cross. The cross is the ultimate exposure of human hatred towards God. On the cross we see ourselves for who we truly are.

When we get the chance, we kill our Creator. That's the message of the parable of the tenants in Mark 12:1–12. An owner leaves his vineyard in the care of tenants. But when he sends servants to collect some of the fruit, they repeatedly beat the servants and send them back empty-handed. Jesus says with heavy poignancy: 'He had one left to send, a son, whom he loved. He sent him last of all, saying, "They will respect my son"' (6). But the tenants say, 'This is the heir. Come, let's kill him, and the inheritance will be ours'

(7). Jesus is that Son whom the Father loves. And he stands before humanity, sent by the Father, looking for the fruit of obedience. In the parable, the tenants 'took him and killed him, and threw him out of the vineyard' (8). And with tragic irony the religious leaders respond to the parable by plotting to kill the Son. They reveal the hearts of us all. We live our lives without God. We push him out of our world and onto the cross.

The cross reveals divine judgment

The cross represents human rebellion and evil. But it also reveals God's response to our rebellion. We see God's judgment against our sin, and his curse on creation. Jesus is not only forsaken by humanity. He's also forsaken by God. Karl Barth said: 'The "for us" of his death on the cross included and encloses this terrible "against us".'[31] This is the reality of history. Our world has been cursed by God. It is out of joint. It is a world of pain, decay, suffering and death.

A new beginning

When Jesus rose from the dead, he rose for us, and not only for us, but for all creation. As a result of humanity's fall into sin, this world has become a place of sickness and decay and death. History has become a time of suffering and frustration and fear. But Christ's resurrection was the beginning of a new era – a new history. The new age has begun in the midst of the old.

The significance of the resurrection is not simply that someone rose from the dead – that had happened before. Nor is it simply that someone rose from the dead never to die again – though that was part of it. The resurrection doesn't simply mean *escape* from this fallen world. The resurrection means that this fallen world, with its fallen history, will be redeemed and renewed. The significance of the resurrection lies in the fact that the One who rose was the One who was crucified. 'Don't be alarmed,' says the angel to the woman at the tomb, 'You are looking for Jesus the Nazarene, who was crucified. He has risen!' (Mark 16:6). The One who is risen is the One who cried out: 'My God, why have you forsaken me?' It's the One who died bearing our sin and the godforsakenness that our sin entails. The One who summed up human rebellion and divine judgment is the One who has now risen again. All that characterizes life in this fallen world was borne by him on the cross and overcome. This means the resurrection takes the form of a promise. It's the promise that what has happened to Christ will happen to all creation.

The resurrection was an historical event. It's important for Christians to affirm this. We're not talking about a myth or an ideal, but a real event. Otherwise we're left with a vague optimism without substance or an ethereal hope that doesn't help in the midst of suffering and injustice. This was a real physical, bodily resurrection in the midst of history that promises real physical, bodily renewal at the end of history.

But in one sense the resurrection wasn't an historical event: it was an eschatological event. It wasn't an event in history so much as the beginning of a new history. That's why it doesn't fit into any of our categories. It was never meant to. It was meant to blow those categories apart. We live in an age characterized by the cross: by judgment and curse, by decay and death. The resurrection of Jesus is the start of a whole new world, a world of life and hope and joy. People reject the historical evidence for the resurrection because, they say, resurrections don't happen in our world. But that's the point.

The resurrection of Jesus is the start of a whole new world, a world of life and hope and joy.

They don't. Death happens in our world. But the resurrection of Jesus is the beginning of the renewal of this world, the beginning of new categories, of new hope.

So the cross and resurrection are not simply events that touch the lives of those individuals who turn to Christ in faith. Neither are they simply the means by which Christians escape this fallen world. The cross and resurrection are the fulcrum of history, the point on which it turns. Indeed, they reach out beyond history and touch eternity. They are truly eschatological events. Time and space turn on the cross and resurrection of Jesus. The world is the spatial location for humanity, and history is the temporal location for humanity. Fallen space and fallen time come to their climax in the cross. In the resurrection they are overcome and renewed.

But only a beginning

So the resurrection is a new beginning. Jesus is the firstfruits of a new creation, of renewal, of liberation. But the resurrection of Jesus is only the beginning. We're still awaiting the liberation of creation and the redemption of our bodies. 'The creation *waits* in eager expectation for the sons of God to be revealed . . . the creation *will be* liberated from its bondage to decay and brought into the glorious freedom of the children of God' (Romans 8:19–21; see also Acts 3:21). We're still hoping. Still looking forward. 'Hope that is seen is no hope at all. Who hopes for what he already has? But if we hope for what we do not yet have, we wait for it patiently' (Romans 8:24–25).

Jesus said that all authority had been given to him. But we don't yet see it. Pick up a newspaper. Is the authority of Jesus written across every page? No. We see sin, suffering and evil. We see a world in rebellion against God and a world under the judgment of God. It hardly needs to be proved that the present is unredeemed. The empirical evidence is overwhelming. Conflict. Pollution. Illness. Hatred. Crime. Family break-up. All bear witness that creation is not yet redeemed.

The shadow of the cross

So the cross remains the mark of this age. Its shadow hangs over everything. This is what we're like. This is what our world is like. It's a world of sin and judgment. Alister McGrath says: 'The cross . . . remains the key to our earthly Christian existence . . . It is the cross, interpreted in the light of the resurrection, which must remain the key to our understanding of this world and our destiny within it. Christian existence in general, and Christian *discipleship* in particular, are governed by the cross.'[32]

Yes, we should work against poverty. Yes, we should try to avoid tragedies. Of course we should. We're people of the cross. We embrace sacrificial love and the service of others. We, of all people, will be concerned for those who suffer. The patience of hope is always connected with the work of faith and labour of love (1 Thessalonians 1:3).

But we're also people who know, as the Book of Common Prayer puts it, that 'in the midst of life we are in death'. We know that the justice of God's reign and the renewal of all things can't be achieved by us in history.

The cross is the mark of history; the resurrection is the mark of God's new future. The cross is the mark of the present; the resurrection is the mark of the future. The cross is the mark of the broken earth; the resurrection is the mark of the new earth. The pattern of cross–resurrection is the pattern for all of space and time. It is, as Paul puts it, 'bondage to decay' in the present, followed by liberation into 'glorious freedom' in the future (Romans 8:21).

And why does this matter?

It gives us robust realism in the present

This expectation of bondage followed by freedom enables us to be realistic about the present. We expect work to be frustrating. We expect our bodies to decay. We expect relationships to go through conflict.

Or at least we ought to expect these things.

The young man and woman snuggled up together on the sofa. The room was full of people, but they were oblivious to everyone else. He was everything she had ever hoped for. She was everything he needed. And soon they would be married. Three months later, when they asked to talk with me, it was a different story. Married life hadn't been 'happy ever after'. They were, after all, two sinners, saved by grace but not yet transformed, thrown into close proximity. Of course there would be problems. Of course there would be conflict. They were bound to threaten each other's idols. Indeed, they *were* each other's idol. But idols always disappoint. Their hopes for married life were so high that there could only be a let-down. It felt like a disaster. But it was just normal life in a fallen world.

I remember talking to a colleague in the canteen at work whose best friend was dying of cancer. Kathy and Emma shared a flat together, and so day after day Kathy witnessed Emma in terrible pain. A tragedy. Kathy was being told by people in her church that God would heal her friend if only she prayed in faith. But Emma hadn't been healed and her life was clearly ebbing away. Kathy had been promised resurrection change in this life, but witnessed only the shadow of the cross. A double tragedy. Not only was there the trauma of Emma's deterioration, but Kathy's faith was shaken. Was God unable to keep his promises? Or was he indifferent to her cries? Or was it her faith that was inadequate?

> For us, death at a young age – or even anytime before our late 60s or so – seems to be an abnormal tragedy. If a relative dies young, we do not merely grieve; our lives are devastated. We question the existence of God . . . Though we entertain ourselves with a constant stream of simulated violence on TV, if we witness a real killing, or a battle, we are far more prone than traditional people to suffer mental or emotional breakdown. We are less resilient than our forebears.[33]

A friend's wife died in her mid-sixties after a terminal illness. My friend complained bitterly about the doctors: 'They ought to be able to do something.' Our culture expects so much as a right and complains bitterly when life doesn't deliver. Health. Good looks. Education. Work. Prosperity. Holidays. Sex. Entertainment. We expect to be cured. We want cosmetic surgery. Every child should get good grades. Every tragedy should be averted. Someone should give me a job. If I can't afford something, then I'll get it on credit. I deserve it. I need it. I have a right to it.

Here's what we have a right to: hell. Anything else is a bonus. So accept health and partial health, prosperity and making do, work and social benefits, holidays and days at home, as good, gracious, undeserved gifts from God. Enjoy them. Don't moan about what you haven't got. Enjoy all that God has given. You don't deserve it. You deserve hell. Life on earth is a bonus. Life in the new earth will be heaven!

It gives us robust hope for the future

Tony Campolo describes a church meeting he attended led by an old African-American pastor:

> He started his sermon real softly by saying, 'It was Friday; it was Friday and my Jesus was dead on the tree. But that was Friday,

and Sunday's comin'!' One of the Deacons yelled, 'Preach, brother, preach!' It was all the encouragement he needed. He came on louder as he said, 'It was Friday and Mary was cryin' her eyes out. The disciples were runnin' in every direction, like sheep without a shepherd, but that was Friday, and Sunday's comin!'

The preacher kept going. He picked up the volume still more and shouted, 'It was Friday. The cynics were lookin' at the world and sayin' "As things have been so shall they be. You can't change anything in this world; you can't change anything." But those cynics don't know that it was only Friday. Sunday's comin'! It was Friday, and on Friday those forces that oppress the poor and make the poor to suffer were in control. But that was Friday! Sunday's comin'!

It was Friday, and on Friday Pilate thought he had washed his hands of a lot of trouble. The Pharisees were struttin' around, laughin' and pokin' each other in the ribs. They thought they were back in charge of things. But they didn't know it was only Friday! Sunday's comin'!

He kept on working that one phrase for a half hour, then an hour, then an hour and a quarter, then an hour and a half. Over and over he came at us, 'It's Friday, but Sunday's comin!' By the time he had come to the end of the message . . . he had me and everybody else so worked up that I don't think any of us could have stood it much longer. At the end of his message he just yelled at the top of his lungs, 'It's FRIDAY!' and all 500 of us in that church yelled back with one accord, 'SUNDAY'S COMIN'!'[34]

11. HIDDENNESS FOLLOWED BY REVELATION – THE PATTERN FOR THE KINGDOM

We commonly speak of the return of Christ. The New Testament, however, more often uses the language of 'revelation'.[35]

> But the day Lot left Sodom, fire and sulphur rained down from heaven and destroyed them all. It will be just like this on the day the Son of Man is *revealed*.
> (Luke 17:29–30)

> . . . as you eagerly wait for our Lord Jesus Christ to be *revealed*.
> (1 Corinthians 1: 7)

> This will happen when the Lord Jesus is *revealed* from heaven in blazing fire with his powerful angels.
> (2 Thessalonians 1:7)

> . . . *he will appear a second time*, not to bear sin, but to bring salvation to those who are waiting for him.
> (Hebrews 9:28)

> In his great mercy he has given us new birth into a living hope . . . who through faith are shielded by God's power until the coming of the salvation that is ready to be *revealed* in the last time. In this you greatly rejoice, though now for a little while you may have had to suffer grief in all kinds of trials. These have come so that your faith – of greater worth than gold, which perishes even though refined by fire – may be proved genuine and may result in praise, glory and honour when Jesus Christ is *revealed*.
> (1 Peter 1:3–7)

> And now, dear children, continue in him, so that when *he appears* we may be confident and unashamed before him at his coming.
> (1 John 2:28)

Alongside the idea of future revelation is the idea of present hiddenness.

> At that time Jesus, full of joy through the Holy Spirit, said, 'I praise you, Father, Lord of heaven and earth, because you have *hidden* these things from the wise and learned, and *revealed* them to little children. Yes, Father, for this was your good pleasure.'
> (Luke 10:21)

> For whatever is *hidden* is meant to be *disclosed*, and whatever is *concealed* is meant to be *brought out into the open*.
> (Mark 4:22; see also Luke 8:17)

> For you died, and your life is now *hidden* with Christ in God. When Christ, who is your life, *appears*, then you also will *appear* with him in glory.
> (Colossians 3:3–4)

The secret kingdom

This is how we're to understand the parables of the kingdom. Jesus begins his ministry by announcing the coming of God's kingdom. We see his royal authority over sickness, sin, the spirit world, the natural world and even over death. Yet he's also opposed and rejected. This isn't what the Jews expected of God's kingdom. They expected it to come in a great blaze of glory. Even John the Baptist begins to have his doubts over whether Jesus can be the real thing (Matthew 11:2–3).

Jesus responds in the parables of the kingdom by saying that the kingdom comes in two stages. First, the kingdom comes secretly. The Jews expected that the kingdom would come in triumph. God would sweep away his enemies. But the secret of the kingdom is that, even though this hasn't yet happened, the kingdom has genuinely come. It has come secretly. It has come in a hidden way. Like a proverbial mustard seed, it is small and seemingly insignificant (Mark 4:30-31). The secret of the kingdom is that it's a secret: that it's here even though it doesn't look like it's here (4:11).

It comes secretly because it comes graciously. In the book of Malachi, the people complain, 'Where is the God of justice?' (Malachi 2:17). Malachi says: 'The Lord you are seeking will come . . . But who can endure the day of his coming?' (3:1–2). When the God of justice comes in triumph and judgment he will come down your street. He will judge you, and who can stand in the face of his judgment? This is the dilemma of God's people: we long for God to intervene in justice and establish his rule. But his coming will be *our* defeat and *our* judgment. The solution is that the coming of God's kingdom takes place in two stages. First, he comes secretly and graciously. There is judgment, but the King is the one who is judged. Judgment takes place at the cross and it falls on the King in our place. The kingdom comes, at first, in grace. And it comes through the word (Mark 4:14). The kingdom grows when people 'hear and accept' the word of God (4:20). In Jesus the kingdom of God comes in a gracious way through the gospel as the gift of salvation and the call to repentance.

But the Jews weren't wrong in their expectations. The kingdom *will* come in glory and power and judgment. We shouldn't think that the secret, gracious presence of the kingdom means the kingdom won't one day come in triumph. The seed grows all but unnoticed (4:26–29). The hidden kingdom remains hidden in history. But grow it does, until there's a great harvest. The kingdom may be secret, hidden, opposed, rejected. But make no mistake: it will come in glory, offering refuge to people from throughout the world (4:30–32). '"Do you bring in a lamp to put it under a bowl or a bed?" asks Jesus. "Instead, don't you put it on its stand? For whatever is hidden is meant to be disclosed, and whatever is concealed is meant to be brought out into the open"' (4:21–22). One day, the secret kingdom will be disclosed. The word 'apocalypse' means 'revelation'. So, says Jesus, get ready. For some, this will mean salvation and glory; for others, it will mean judgment and defeat (Matthew 13:24–30, 36–43).

Think about Mark's readers. They were told that Jesus had risen in triumph, had ascended to the right hand of God, had been given all authority. And yet life just went on the same: buying and selling, giving birth and growing old. Ordinary. All very ordinary. Worse than that. They faced opposition, rejection and apathy. Just like us.

We live in a world in which the words 'Jesus is King' seem

out of place. But the kingdom of God is here. It's here in a hidden form through the word of God. It's here in a gracious form in the new people of God. We are the kingdom community which makes God's reign visible in the world. The kingdom is not 'spiritual' (as opposed to 'earthly'); it's hidden. The sixteenth-century theologian John Calvin said that the kingdom 'has not been made clearly manifest; rather it lies in the shadow of the cross and is violently opposed by [Christ's] enemies'.[36] But what is currently hidden will one day be revealed. One day the glory of God will fill the earth as the waters cover the sea.

What is currently hidden will one day be revealed. One day the glory of God will fill the earth as the waters cover the sea.

Mission and the cross[37]

The essential mark of Christian mission in the world is the cross. Mission takes place in the power of the Spirit , but it is characterized by service and love. It is conducted with gentleness and respect. Missiologist David Smith asks: 'As an evangelical who wishes to confess the centrality of the cross in discipleship, theology and mission, I find myself asking whether, despite all our protestations that the death of Christ lies at the heart of our understanding of the Gospel, we have not treated it in ways that have eroded its power and glory.'[38]

In the mission of the cross there's no place for 'power evangelism' – aggressive and manipulative methods of persuasion. Our reliance isn't on persuasive arguments or polished performances or material incentives. Paul explicitly rejected such approaches: 'My message and my preaching were not with wise and persuasive words.' 'We have renounced secret and shameful ways; we do not use deception, nor do we distort the word of God.' Instead we set 'forth the truth plainly', relying on 'the Spirit's power' (1 Corinthians 2:4; 2 Corinthians 4:2). Our message is 'Christ crucified: a stumbling-block to Jews and foolishness to Gentiles, but to those whom God has called, both Jews and Greeks, Christ the power of God and the wisdom of God' (1 Corinthians 1:23–24). What persuades others is not our dynamic personalities, nor our clever arguments, but the illumination of the Spirit (1 Corinthians 2:6–16). Asian theologian Kosuke Koyama talks about a 'crucified mind' which approaches others with self-denial, compassion and humility.

In the mission of the cross there's no place for 'power profiles'. We easily think that what matters is what has profile, what's seen, what's written and talked about. We want media attention, national campaigns, celebrity endorsement. Don Carson says:

> Why is it that we constantly parade Christian athletes, media personalities and pop singers? Why should we think their opinions or their experience of grace are of any more significance than those of any other believer? When we tell outsiders about people in our church, do we instantly think of the despised and the lowly who have become Christians, or do we love to impress people with the importance of men and women who have become Christians? Modern Western evangelicalism is deeply infected with the virus of triumphalism and the resulting illness destroys humility, minimizes grace, and offers far too much homage to money and influence and 'wisdom of our day'.[39]

In the mission of the cross, there's no place for 'power politics' in which Christians think they can promote the cause of Christ through legislation. Yes, we need to be socially involved as an expression of our love for our neighbours. But our concern will be other people rather than self-interest.

Our concern will be social justice rather than the imposition of Christian values through state power. Christ's kingdom is extended through his word and in his community. It's not extended through the laws of the state. In response to those who wanted to progress the Reformation through force, Martin Luther preached eight *Invocavit Sermons*. He said:

> It is not in my power or hand to fashion the hearts of men as the potter moulds the clay and fashions them at his pleasure. I can get no farther than their ears; their hearts I cannot reach . . . That is God's work alone, who causes faith to live in the heart. Therefore we should give free course to the word and not add our works to it . . . I simply taught, preached and wrote God's word; otherwise I did nothing. And while I slept, or drank Wittenberg beer with my friends . . . the word so greatly weakened the papacy that no prince or emperor ever inflicted such losses upon it. I did nothing; the word did everything.[40]

In the mission of the cross, there's no place for 'power strategies' in which Christians rely on sociological techniques for church growth. Size matters to us. Big churches. Big organizations. Big events. This is the spirit of our culture. It's not the way of the cross. Jesus says the kingdom grows unseen. The Father has given the kingdom to Christ's 'little flock' (Luke 12:32). We think the megachurches, national conferences, platform speakers are where it's at. But Jesus says the kingdom has been given to his little flock: to countless small congregations, among the poor and marginalized, to faithful Christians serving quietly, away from the limelight. Mark Thompson comments: 'Perhaps we need to be particularly vigilant that we do not simply reflect the assessment of the pagan world around us, applauding the spectacular, pursuing impact and the trappings of success, and despising the so-called weakness of an unadorned ministry of prayer and the word of God.'[41]

The Latin American missiologist Samuel Escobar calls on us to abandon 'the imperial mission mentality' which carries out 'missionary work from a position of superiority: political, military, financial, technological'.[42]

When my daughter Katie accompanied me to Uganda, she needed an injection to protect her against yellow fever. When she came home from the clinic, her mum asked, 'Did it hurt? Did you bleed? Show me where the needle went in.' Her focus was on the needle, on the wound, on the place that was bleeding. That was where a difference could be seen. But what protected Katie from disease was not the plaster on her arm, but the vaccine moving unseen around her body. Jesus said the kingdom of God is like yeast in dough. What matters is not what can be seen, but the unseen work of God's people and God's word. Denominations, missionary agencies, national campaigns, parachurch bodies – all have a profile and so we can easily think they're what matters. But it's not true. I'm sure they have a supporting role. But what really matters in God's kingdom are small, local churches faithfully proclaiming God's word and serving their communities.

A church of the cross

Martin Luther distinguished between theologies of glory and a theology of the cross.[43] Theologies of glory seek the revelation of God in the power and glory of his actions. It is proud theology that claims knowledge of God through human wisdom. The theology of the cross sees the ultimate revelation of God in the cross. Knowledge of God is hidden so that it is only known through humility and faith. It is hidden in what is contrary. Only by faith can we see in the cross: power in weakness, wisdom in foolishness and glory in shame.

We need to develop a corresponding understanding of *the church of the cross.*[44] A church of glory believes that God uses the powerful and important and impressive. But God chooses the poor, weak and foolish to confound the privileged, influential and powerful (1 Corinthians 1:26–31). This is what the Reformers meant when they spoke of the kingdom as 'hidden in the cross and in what is contrary'.[45] The transforming power and rule of God are present now in a hidden way in the lives of believers and in the Christian community.

This should fill us with humility. But it should also fill us with enthusiasm and expectancy. The great commission won't be accomplished by self-important institutions, consultants, networks and conferences. It will be fulfilled by hundreds and thousands of small, struggling churches. People like you and me. Unseen. Unnoticed. But all the time, the kingdom is growing secretly until the day it is revealed in glory. 'Therefore we do not lose heart' (2 Corinthians 4:16).

12. SUFFERING FOLLOWED BY GLORY – THE PATTERN FOR DISCIPLES

We have a right to total victory. I want you to get that down on the inside. Not partial victory to where we have a good family, we have good health, but we constantly struggle in our finances. That's not total victory . . . Maybe God has blessed you. You have a good family, a good job, but you've had pain in your body for years and years. You used to stand against it. You used to believe you could be free. But now it's been so long you've just decided 'This is my lot in life. Joel, this is my cross to carry' . . . Let me assure you, he didn't create you to be average. He didn't create you to barely get by, to have all kinds of things holding you back. You've got to get the right vision. God created you to be totally free, to have peace in your mind, to walk in divine health, to have good relationships, to have plenty to pay your bills. God created us as victors and not victims. Fight the good fight of faith. Know who you are, the seed of Abraham. You have rights and privileges. One of those privileges is total victory.

So says Joel Osteen, best-selling author, preaching to his mega-church in Texas. But can Christians live in total victory?

We've seen how the pattern of the cross and resurrection – the pattern of suffering followed by glory – was not only the pattern for Jesus, but is also the pattern for the world. The pattern of the cross and resurrection applies in the same way to believers. We follow the way of the cross. The cross is the essential mark of Christian discipleship. We follow the way of the cross, not the way of glory. But we follow the way of the cross sustained by the hope of coming glory. The pattern of Christian experience conforms to the pattern of Christ's own experience. The way of the cross is followed by the glory of the resurrection. Suffering followed by glory.

In Acts 13 – 14, Luke describes how Paul and Barnabas planted churches in Pisidian Antioch, Iconium and Lystra on the outward leg of their first missionary journey, before ending up in Derbe. Then they came back again through Lystra, Iconium and Antioch (14:21). Luke tells us they returned, 'strengthening the disciples and encouraging them to remain true to the faith'. What would you say to strengthen and encourage brand new churches? What are the important truths they need to hear? This is how Luke summarizes the words of Paul and Barnabas: 'We must go through many hardships to enter the kingdom of God' (22). Suffering followed by glory. This is basic Christianity.

Many of those new believers would have been Jewish. They expected the coming of the Messiah to usher in God's kingdom along with the defeat of God's enemies and the vindication of God's people. Now the Messiah had come. The new age had begun. But God's people were still hard-pressed. This they didn't expect! They needed to know that the sufferings they were facing didn't negate the message they'd heard. The kingdom had come now in a hidden way and only in the future would it come in a glorious way. In the meantime, God's people would have to go through many hardships.

We find this suffering–glory pattern running through Paul's theology. In Romans 8 he says, 'We share in [Christ's] sufferings in order that we may also share in his glory. I consider that our present sufferings are not worth comparing with the glory that will be revealed in us' (Romans 8:17–18). The pattern of suffering followed by glory is a pattern we share with Christ. And it's a necessary pattern: we share in the sufferings of Christ *in order that* we might share in his glory. The point is not that we earn glory by suffering. The point is that there's no other road to glory except the Jerusalem road.

It's because of this suffering–glory pattern that Paul can argue that suffering leads ultimately to hope. The experience of suffering is a confirmation that we will share in 'the hope of the glory of God' (Romans 5:2–4). In the light of such hope, Paul can say that 'just as the sufferings of Christ flow over into our lives, so also through Christ our comfort overflows' (2 Corinthians 1:5, 7). Richard Bauckham comments:

> Paul's experience might often seem outwardly unremarkable. But because he sees the death and resurrection of Jesus as the key to his life, as to everything else, he can find there a pattern which makes Christian sense of his experience. The shape which everyone needs to give to his experience in order to understand it Paul found in the cross and resurrection of Jesus . . . All the ups and downs of his ministry were for Paul experiences *of God*, events in which he experienced an identification with Jesus in his dying and rising.[46]

The writer of Hebrews commends to us the faith of 'the cloud of witnesses' from the Old Testament. Their faith is defined as 'being sure of what we hope for and certain of what we do not see' (Hebrews 11:1). These were people who lived sacrificially in the present because of their confidence in the glorious future that God promises. It's the suffering–glory pattern again. The climax of the section is the example of Jesus himself 'who for the joy set before him endured the cross, scorning its shame, and sat down at the right hand of the throne of God' (12:2). There again is the pattern of suffering followed by glory, shame followed by joy, the cross followed by enthronement. This is our model and inspiration: 'Consider him who endured such opposition from sinful men, so that you will not grow weary and lose heart' (12:3).

This pattern of suffering followed by glory also runs throughout 1 Peter. We've already seen the way Peter calls us to the way of the cross. 'To this you were called, because Christ suffered for you, leaving you an example, that you should follow in his steps' (1 Peter 2:21). The cross is the model for citizens (2:13–17) and slaves (2:18–25), for wives and husbands (3:1–7), and for all Christians in their suffering (3:8–22). But this call to the way of the cross is set in a bigger context – the pattern of suffering followed by glory.

Peter refers to Christians as 'aliens and strangers' (1:1; 2:11). Our present experience is one of alienation and dislocation because we've become citizens of God's coming world. We're looking forward to a new home: 'a new heaven and a new earth, the home of righteousness' (2 Peter 3:13). We've been given 'new birth into a living hope', a future 'inheritance'. Meanwhile in the present we rejoice in this hope while we 'suffer grief in all kinds of trials' (1 Peter 1:3–6). Suffering followed by glory.

The Spirit of God in the prophets was predicting 'the sufferings of Christ and the glories that would follow' (1:11). In other words, the (Old Testament) Scriptures point to this pattern of suffering followed by glory. Now the pattern of suffering and glory in the experience of Christ has become the experience of all believers as we participate with Christ.

> Dear friends, do not be surprised at the painful trial you are suffering, as though something strange were happening to you. But rejoice that you participate in the sufferings of Christ, so that you may be overjoyed when his glory is revealed.
> (1 Peter 4:12–13)

> To the elders among you, I appeal as a fellow-elder, a witness of Christ's sufferings and one who also will share in the glory to be revealed: Be shepherds of God's flock that is under your care, serving as overseers – not because you must, but because you are willing, as God wants you to be; not greedy for money, but eager to serve; not lording it over those entrusted to you, but being examples to the flock. And when the Chief Shepherd appears, you will receive the crown of glory that will never fade away.
> (1 Peter 5:1–4)

> Young men, in the same way be submissive to those who are older. All of you, clothe yourselves with humility towards one another, because, 'God opposes the proud but gives grace to the humble.' Humble yourselves, therefore, under God's mighty hand, that he may lift you up in due time.
> (1 Peter 5:5–6)

We can rejoice in sufferings because, as we participate in the sufferings of Christ, we find assurance that we'll participate in the glory of Christ. Peter appeals to leaders on the basis that he is a witness of Christ's suffering and glory. Why does he appeal to them in this way? Because this is to be their pattern. They're to serve, willingly and selflessly, following the model laid down by Christ (Mark 10:42–45). But they do this in the hope of a 'crown of glory that will never fade away'. As Christians, we are to humble ourselves so that God might lift us up. Humility followed by exaltation. Suffering followed by glory.

One dimension of this pattern is that of submission followed by vindication. Christ submitted to his unjust sufferings, trusting himself to God (1 Peter 2:23), and as a result he was vindicated by God (3:17–22). Likewise, Christians are to entrust themselves to God, confident in future glory (4:12–19). 'If you are insulted because of the name of Christ, you are blessed, for the Spirit of glory and of God rests on you' (1 Peter 4:14).

Peter concludes by saying that he has written, 'encouraging you and testifying that this is the true grace of God' (5:12). What is this true grace of God? The preceding verses say: 'And the God of all grace, who called you to his eternal glory in Christ, after you have suffered a little while, will himself restore you and make you strong, firm and steadfast. To him be the power for ever and ever. Amen' (1 Peter 5:10–11) The true grace of God, the grace that makes him 'the God of all grace', consists of this: he has called us to eternal glory after we've suffered a little while. Suffering followed by glory.

Peter needs to write to confirm that this is the *true* grace of God because then, as now, there are *false* versions of grace. Such versions of grace promise glory now or glory without suffering.

- It's a false grace of God when Christians claim they can leave behind the struggle with sin, and live a higher life resting on God.
- It's a false grace of God when Christians claim they can leave behind struggles of sickness, and claim full and unbroken health.

- It's a false grace of God when Christians claim they can leave behind the struggles and humility of mission, and claim victory over people and areas.
- It's a false grace of God when Christians claim they can leave behind suffering and sacrifice, and claim prosperity.
- It's a false grace of God when Christians claim they can leave behind the hiddenness of God's kingdom, and complete the task of mission through grand buildings, political influence, dynamic strategies, global structures, charismatic personalities or megachurches.

An eschatology of the cross

As we saw in the last chapter, the great Reformer Martin Luther distinguished between what he called theologies of glory and a theology of the cross. Theologies of glory seek to know God through human reflection on the power and glory of his actions, while a theology of the cross sees the ultimate revelation of God in the cross. On the cross, faith sees power in weakness, victory in failure and glory in shame.

In the same way, we need to distinguish between eschatologies of glory and an eschatology of the cross.[47] Eschatologies of glory seek the glory and victory of the resurrection without accepting the reality of the cross in the present. But an eschatology of the cross looks forward to glory and victory, but recognizes that in the present they're hidden in shame and weakness.

The eschatology of the cross recognizes that the kingdom of God is hidden now and that its glory lies in the future. Eschatologies of glory, in contrast, expect the glory that belongs to the future to come now, in the present. They expect to move beyond the sacrifice, suffering and submission of the cross to perfection, glory and triumph. They want power and status and honour in the present.

John Calvin says the fault of the disciples was 'to confuse the completeness of Christ's kingdom with its beginning, and to wish to acquire on earth what should be sought in heaven'. Calvin comments, 'It is enough that the faithful receive a taste of these good things now, that they may cherish the hope of their full enjoyment in the future.'[48] He speaks of hope not only sustaining faith, but also restraining it.[49] The very fact that we hope reminds us that we haven't yet received our full redemption (Romans 8:24–25).

John Calvin says the fault of the disciples was 'to confuse the completeness of Christ's kingdom with its beginning, and to wish to acquire on earth what should be sought in heaven'.

Again and again in the New Testament, alongside hope we find patience and long-suffering.

> For in this hope we were saved. But hope that is seen is no hope at all. Who hopes for what he already has? But if we hope for what we do not yet have, *we wait for it patiently.*
> (Romans 8:24–25)

> *Be joyful in hope, patient in affliction*, faithful in prayer.
> (Romans 12:12)

> *Be patient*, then, brothers, until the Lord's coming. See how the farmer waits for the land to yield its valuable crop and how patient he is for the autumn and spring rains. You too, *be patient* and stand firm, because the Lord's coming is near.
> (James 5:7–8)

> Since you have kept my command *to endure patiently*, I will also keep you from the hour of trial that is going to come upon the whole world to test those who live on the earth.
> (Revelation 3:10; see also 1:9; 2:2, 19)

But patience and long-suffering are not common characteristics among Western Christians. Modern Westerners expect good health as a norm. We call for public inquiries because we think every disaster can be avoided. And Christians are not so very different. We expect God to keep us healthy and safe. So when trouble comes – as Jesus promises it will (John 16:33) – we not only struggle to cope with the problem; we also can't make sense of what God is doing. 'Why doesn't he answer my prayers?' 'Is my faith too weak?' The result is that people struggling with turmoil in their circumstances are beset at the same time with turmoil in their hearts – a crisis that could have been avoided by a proper eschatology. Commenting on Hebrews 11:1, Calvin writes:

> Eternal life is promised to us, but it is promised to the dead; we are told of the resurrection of the blessed, but meantime we are involved in corruption; we are declared to be just, and sin dwells within us; we hear that we are blessed, but meantime we are overwhelmed by untold miseries; we are promised an abundance of all good things, but we are often hungry and thirsty; God proclaims that he will come to us immediately, but seems to be deaf to our cries. What would happen to us if we did not rely on hope, and if our minds did not emerge above the world out of the midst of darkness through the shining Word of God and by his Spirit?[50]

Anne Steele (1716–1778) lost her mother when she was just three years old. At nineteen, she had a severe hip injury which made her a lifelong invalid. Then when she was twenty-one, her fiancé drowned the day before they were to be married. This woman, whose life was touched by so much tragedy, wrote:

Thou lovely source of true delight,
whom I unseen adore,
unveil thy beauties to my sight
that I might love thee more.

Thy glory o'er creation shines,
but in thy sacred Word
I read in fairer, brighter lines
my bleeding, dying Lord.

'Tis here, whene'er my comforts droop
and sin and sorrow rise,
thy love with cheering beams of hope
my fainting heart supplies.

But ah! Too soon the pleasing scene
is clouded o'er with pain.
My gloomy fears rise dark between
and I again complain.

Jesus, my Lord, my life, my light,
oh come with blissful ray.
Break radiant through the shades of night
and chase my fears away.

Then shall my soul with rapture trace
the wonders of thy love.
But the full glories of thy face
are only known above.

Betty Carlson tells the story of her friend, Gladys, who has spent the last few years bed-bound. 'From this unique pulpit,' writes Carlson, 'she carries on a more spirited mission programme than many entire churches.' Unable to sleep, she corresponds with missionaries around the world in the early hours. Their neighbour sees the light in her window when he goes out to milk his cows. 'Well, I see Gladys is writing letters again,' he often comments to Gladys's husband. 'Gladys has accepted this as a gift of God to be able to encourage others,' comments Carlson. 'Rather than lie sleepless and concentrate on her pain and other problems, she has learned that the hours pass quickly when thinking of others. Rarely do her letters mention her illness. Actually they are hymns of praise to God, her Lord and Saviour, who has reached down and given her happiness and an overflowing heart in the midst of her personal difficulties.'[51]

Peter describes our trials as being for 'a little while' (1 Peter 1:6). Paul says our troubles are 'light and momentary' (2 Corinthians 4:17). Both Peter and Paul were imprisoned and probably martyred. So they weren't being flippant. By our standards their trials were heavy and sustained. But imagine looking back after a million, billion years of eternal glory. Then our trials will indeed seem light and momentary. Paul says:

> Therefore we do not lose heart. Though outwardly we are wasting away, yet inwardly we are being renewed day by day. For our light and momentary troubles are achieving for us an eternal glory that far outweighs them all. So we fix our eyes not on what is seen, but on what is unseen. For what is seen is temporary, but what is unseen is eternal.
> (2 Corinthians 4:16–18)

Part Four:
The power of the resurrection – power to be weak

The experience of resurrection is not only in the future. We have resurrection power, freedom and life now, through the Holy Spirit. Through the Spirit, we enjoy a foretaste of the life of the age to come. But we have power to be weak, freedom to serve, life to die. The Spirit helps us live the way of the cross. Our hidden life is revealed in our conformity to the cross.

13. RESURRECTION POWER, FREEDOM AND LIFE

'I know he will rise again in the resurrection at the last day.' So says Martha to Jesus when Jesus tells her that her dead brother, Lazarus, will live (John 11:24). Some Jews at the time of Jesus doubted there was any life after death. But most, like Martha, believed in resurrection at the last day. Some day God would intervene in history, vindicate his people and raise the dead. Some day. Some day at the end of history.

Jesus replies to her: 'I am the resurrection and the life. He who believes in me will live, even though he dies; and whoever lives and believes in me will never die' (25–26). In Jesus, the far-off event of resurrection is about to happen in history. His resurrection will be the beginning of the 'last days'. Martha's expectation is right. There will be a coming resurrection when those who believe will live, even though they've died. But resurrection is about to become a present reality. The future is about to invade history.

We've seen how the Christian life is patterned on the cross

and resurrection. We experience suffering followed by glory, just as in the cross and resurrection we see 'the sufferings of Christ and the glories that would follow' (1 Peter 1:11). We follow the way of the cross in the present with the hope of resurrection glory to come.

But resurrection isn't just a future hope. It's also a present experience.

Resurrection power

> I pray also that the eyes of your heart may be enlightened in order that you may know the hope to which he has called you, the riches of his glorious inheritance in the saints, and his incomparably great power for us who believe. That power is like the working of his mighty strength, which he exerted in Christ when he raised him from the dead and seated him at his right hand in the heavenly realms.
> (Ephesians 1:18–20)

Paul prays that Christians might realize the power that is ours in Christ. It's the same power by which God raised Christ from the dead. On Easter morning, Jesus' body lay dead and lifeless: flesh, rotting into dust. But God reached down and wrenched Jesus from the grave. God did what he did at creation: he brought life where there was no life (Romans 4:17). Death is the one force that no person can escape from or overcome. But on that first Easter day, God took on death and won. He overcame the power of death. Paul talks of God's 'incomparably great power'.

We've seen how the cross is the great declaration of God's love: if ever we have cause to doubt God's intentions, we can look to the cross and see his goodness written large. In a similar way, the resurrection is the great declaration of

God's power. If ever we have cause to doubt God's power, we can look to the resurrection. Peter Hicks says: 'Either the resurrection happened or it did not happen. If it did happen, then it demonstrated once and for all that the power of God is greater than any other power. If ever you begin to doubt God's ability to sort out any and every problem, look again at the resurrection.'[52]

So much for *God's* power. Paul goes further. He says that God's 'incomparably great power' is '*for us* who believe' (Ephesians 1:19). God's resurrection power is at work *within us*. God has seated Christ 'far above all rule and authority, power and dominion' (21). He has 'placed all things under his feet and appointed him to be head over everything' (22). Enthroned above all rule. Placed over all things. Appointed head over all things. And all, says Paul, 'for the church' (22). He wields all power for his church. For us. For you.

Ephesus was a centre for occult activity. Imagine living in a context where the power of evil is palpable. It must have been so intimidating. Maybe that's how you feel – surrounded by alien powers with all sorts of social pressures to conform with the world's way of thinking, to keep quiet about your Christian beliefs, to fit in with what's going on. The power of the world seems so strong. But a much greater power is at work in us and for us, if only we would realize it.

Resurrection power is coursing through your veins. You're like some spiritual superhero with untold power at your disposal. Really, you are.

Resurrection freedom

Not only does the resurrection bring power; it also brings freedom – freedom from the slavery of sin.

> For we know that our old self was crucified with him so that the body of sin might be done away with, that we should no longer be slaves to sin – because anyone who has died has been freed from sin.
>
> Now if we died with Christ, we believe that we will also live with him. For we know that since Christ was raised from the dead, he cannot die again; death no longer has mastery over him. The death he died, he died to sin once for all; but the life he lives, he lives to God.
>
> (Romans 6:6–10)

Because we're united to Christ in his death, his death becomes our death. And that means our old self with its inbuilt bias towards sin was crucified with Christ. It's dead. It's gone. We're set free from its power. And because we're united with Christ in his resurrection, his life becomes our life. We're free to live for God. The bondage of sin is broken and we receive a new life. A revolution has taken place. The old regime of Sin has been toppled. The life-giving reign of Grace has been established in its place.

Think about what happened at your baptism. Your baptism was an eschatological act, marking your move from the old age to the new age. The resurrection of Jesus marked the beginning of the new age. Your resurrection with Jesus, enacted in baptism, marks the beginning of the new age *for you*.

In Romans 5, Paul contrasts the old humanity in Adam with the new humanity in Christ. He contrasts the reign of Sin, which leads to death, with the reign of Grace which leads to life. A new age has dawned in the middle of history through the resurrection. At present, it overlaps with the old age of Sin. But one day it'll be the only show in town. It's with this in mind that Paul moves on to speak of baptism. Baptism represents our death to Sin and its reign (6:3–4). Coming up from the water represents our resurrection into the new age. Now we live under the regime of Grace (6:14). Baptism is a sign in history of the presence of the future. 'The revolutionary new world which has begun in the resurrection of Jesus, the world where Jesus reigns as Lord having won the victory over sin and death, has its front-line outposts in those who in baptism have shared his death and resurrection.'[53]

Resurrection life

There's a life which is given to us at the end of time – the new life of bodily resurrection (John 5:24–25). A rotting, decaying dead body is what sin earns. As the flesh decays and stinks, we see the 'value' of sin, the reward of sin, the true nature of sin. But, if a stinking, rotting body is what sin earns, a glorious resurrection body is what grace gives.

But there's also a life that is given to us now in history when we become Christians. 'As for you, you were dead in your transgressions and sins . . . But because of his great love for us, God, who is rich in mercy, made us alive with Christ even when we were dead in transgressions – it is by grace you have been saved' (Ephesians 2:1, 4–5). One moment we were spiritually dead; the next we were spiritually alive. You may not be able to pinpoint the moment when this took place in your experience – many people experience conversion as a gradual transition. But there was a time when you were dead, closed to God, ignorant of him, hardened against him in rebellion. But now, if you're a Christian, you're alive, open to God, knowing God and known by God, soft-hearted towards him in love. We're no longer spiritually dead. We're alive to God.

In the book of Revelation, John talks about a first death and a second death. The first death is physical, at the end of our earthly lives. We die of illness, old age, accidents, violence. Christians and non-Christians alike will face this first death (unless Christ is revealed in glory before we die). But then there's a second death – the death of eternal separation from God. 'The lake of fire is the second death,' says Revelation 20:14. Christians may experience the first death, but we've been rescued from the second death through the cross. John says: 'Blessed and holy are those who have part in the first resurrection. The second death has no power over them' (Revelation 20:6). Notice that John also talks about a first and second resurrection. The second resurrection is the bodily resurrection to eternal life or eternal death which will take place at the end of time on the day of judgment. The first resurrection is the gift of spiritual life that we receive through the Spirit at conversion.

Resurrection power, resurrection freedom, resurrection life. It adds up to a real experience of God's coming new world future, right here, right now. The resurrection of Jesus meant the age to come had begun in history. And that new age has begun for us.

The imperative of the resurrection[54]

Why do we go and make disciples of all nations? The answer in Matthew 28 is because all authority has been given to the Risen Christ. In raising Jesus from the dead, 'God has made this Jesus, whom you crucified, both Lord and Christ' (Acts 2:36). His resurrection is his enthronement. The trial on earth which declared him to be a blasphemer and traitor has been overturned by the heavenly court of appeal. Jesus is about to ascend, as promised in Daniel 7, to receive from the Ancient of Days 'an everlasting dominion that will not pass away, and his kingdom is one that will never be destroyed'. 'He was given authority, glory and sovereign power,' Daniel says. 'All people, nations and men of every language worshipped him' (Daniel 7:14).

Because Jesus has been given authority over the nations, he sends his disciples out to call on the nations to submit to that authority. He exercises his rule on earth through the proclamation of his word – just as God has always reigned through his word. When we proclaim the gospel, we're heralds or ambassadors of the coming King. It's as if we go to the citizens of a country and say that a king who rightly claims their allegiance is coming. Those who currently rule them are usurpers and tyrants. But the true king is coming and he will be their king.

This is what it means to proclaim the gospel: it's an eschatological message. We declare that Jesus is King and that Jesus will be King. The earliest encapsulation of the Christian message was 'Jesus is Lord' – confessed at a time when the rest of the world was declaring Caesar to be Lord (Romans 10:9). Jesus has been given all authority by the Father and one day every knee will bow before him. If people acknowledge his lordship now, they will experience his coming rule as blessing, life and salvation. If they reject him, they will experience his coming rule as conquest, death and judgment.

We live in a culture where choice is everything and value judgments are relative, a culture in which I decide what is right for me. The declaration of Christ's kingship cuts right across this. We don't invite people to make Jesus their king; we *tell* people that Jesus is their king. We don't invite people to meet Jesus; we *warn* people that they'll meet Jesus as their conquering king. We don't offer people a gospel invitation; we *command* people to repent and submit to the coming king. Of course we do this graciously and gently (1 Peter 3:15). We can't force or manipulate repentance. But one day everyone will bow the knee before Jesus, one way or another (Philippians 2:9–11).

Matthew 28 may be the classic text of mission, but, as Chris Wright emphasizes, the whole Bible is a missionary text.[55] It's a missionary text because it tells this story – the story of God reasserting his rule over the world through the kingship of Jesus. It's all there in Psalm 2, one of the Old Testament passages most often quoted in the New Testament. The psalm begins with humanity, in the form of the kings of the earth, rejecting the rule of God and his anointed one. '"Let us break their chains," they say, "and throw off their fetters"' (3). In Acts 4 the early church identified the cross as the climax of this rebellion against God (Acts 4:25–28).

The reality of God's rule is that it brings freedom, life and peace. But we believe the serpent's lie that God's rule is tyrannical. The kings of the earth speak of breaking chains and throwing off fetters. Moreover, not only do we reject God's rule, but we ourselves rule in the image of Satan's lie rather than in the image of God's rule. Human rule is to a greater or lesser extent tyrannical and corrupt – whether in the home, marketplace or nation. This is significant for mission because it means people hear the good news as bad news. We announce the coming of God's rule – a rule that brings life and freedom. But people hear that announcement as a threat. They reject it in favour of self-rule, believing the lie that self-rule leads to freedom, when in fact it leads to slavery.

From Eden onwards, humanity has rejected God's kingship. But Psalm 2 continues with God declaring that he will reassert his reign over this world through his anointed King (Psalm 2:4–6). God's anointed is the next to speak. He repeats God's promise, echoing the covenant with King David in 2 Samuel 7, that he is God's Son and God will give him the nations as an inheritance (Psalm 2:7–9). The writers of the New Testament saw this promise fulfilled in the resurrection of Jesus (Acts 13:32–33). The Risen Christ is given all authority and enthroned in heaven.

Finally in the Psalm, the people of God speak in the person of the psalmist himself. They call on the nations to serve the LORD and submit to the Son (Psalm 2:10–12). The authority of the Risen King is delegated to his people as they proclaim his rule (Revelation 2:27). This is our missionary message: kiss the Son lest you be destroyed when he comes.

But our message is also: 'Blessed are all who take refuge in him' (Psalm 2:12). For there is a twist in the story. When the king comes, he does not come in triumph and glory. He comes, as we've seen, in a hidden way. The coming of God's King must mean conquest and judgment for all humanity. But first he has come in a hidden, gracious way, receiving judgment in our place as our atoning sacrifice. The beauty of grace is that the King who is our greatest threat himself provides a refuge from himself.

The beauty of grace is that the King who is our greatest threat himself provides a refuge from himself.

Much of our evangelism takes an individual you-and-God approach: you've sinned, your sin cuts you off from God, but Jesus removes the consequences of sin so you can know God again. There's nothing incorrect about this story. But the Bible tells a much bigger, fuller story. It's the story of God creating a new humanity, reasserting his life-giving, liberating rule over the world, and bringing it to a climax in the triumph of his Son and the renewal of creation. The danger of the you-and-God message is that self remains at the centre. I'm the almighty consumer, shopping around for what suits me best, with God providing the best option for my religious life. God serves my spiritual needs while Tesco serves my grocery needs. And the customer is always right.

An eschatological vision, by contrast, puts God firmly at the centre. The gospel tells the story of the kingdom of God.[56] The goal of the story is the glory of God, and the climax of the story is 'God . . . all in all' (1 Corinthians 15:28).

The kingdom of God extends beyond my personal concerns to encompass the renewal of all things. Here is a message of hope for those suffering injustice, inequality and abuse. The final judgment is the ultimate declaration that suffering matters and that evil is unacceptable. That declaration is anticipated in the cross and resurrection. The resurrection is the promise that the godlessness and godforsakenness encapsulated in the cross is not the last word. God's kingdom is coming. Eternal life is coming. A new creation is coming.

14. POWER TO BE WEAK

Resurrection power, resurrection freedom, resurrection life. It's a heady cocktail. Yet this is a daily reality for every Christian.

But the experience of resurrection power, freedom and life is only half the picture. Stop here and your Christian discipleship will go seriously off course.

Let me give four quotations from the New Testament:

> I want to know Christ and the power of his resurrection . . .
> (Philippians 3:10)

> [Christ] lives by God's power . . . by God's power we will live with him . . .
> (2 Corinthians 13:4)

> We pray this in order that you may live a life worthy of the Lord and may please him in every way . . . being strengthened with all

> power according to his glorious might . . .
> (Colossians 1:10–11)

> For God did not give us a spirit of timidity, but a spirit of power, of love and of self-discipline . . .
> (2 Timothy 1:7)

I once saw an advert for a conference quoting the first of these Bible verses. 'I want to know Christ and the power of his resurrection,' the advert read. It promised a time of power and victory. But it's only a half a sentence. It wasn't meant to be read on its own. All these texts contain a wonderful truth: we have Christ's resurrection power in us; we have resurrection freedom and life. But each passage goes on:

> I want to know Christ and the power of his resurrection *and the fellowship of sharing in his sufferings, becoming like him in his death* . . .
> Philippians 3:10)

> For to be sure, *he was crucified in weakness*, yet [Christ] lives by God's power. Likewise, *we are weak in him*, yet by God's power we will live with him *to serve you*.
> (2 Corinthians 13:4)

> We pray this in order that you may live a life worthy of the Lord and may please him in every way . . . being strengthened with all power according to his glorious might *so that you may have great endurance and patience* . . .
> (Colossians 1:10–11)

> For God did not give us a spirit of timidity, but a spirit of power, of love and of self-discipline. *So do not be ashamed* to testify about our Lord, or ashamed of me his prisoner. But *join with me in*

> *suffering for the gospel, by the power of God* . . . (2 Timothy 1:7–8) (Italics mine)

Paul wants to know the power of Christ's resurrection *so that* he can share in Christ's sufferings (Philippians 3:10). I'd like to see an advert for a conference that has 'I want to know the fellowship of sharing in Christ's sufferings' emblazoned across it! We have power *so that* we can be weak and put ourselves in a position of humble service (2 Corinthians 13:4). Paul prays that the Colossians might be strengthened with all power *so that* they may have great endurance and patience (Colossians 1:10–11). We have a spirit of power, yes. But we have power *so that* we might suffer for the gospel. And so Timothy is invited to suffer for the gospel 'by the power of God' (2 Timothy 1:8).

To serve, to endure, to suffer, to love. This isn't the language of triumphalism, nor of victory. But it is the language of resurrection power.

Resurrection power means to be like Christ in his death. It is power to be weak. Power to endure. Power to suffer. That's true Christian experience. Power in weakness is our boast.

A few years ago, I visited Uganda to lecture on these themes. When I arrived, there were posters around Kampala advertising a Christian event that promised 'five days of power'. Each day on the way to the college, I passed 'the miracle cathedral' with its promise of unqualified success and freedom. I began my lectures in the Kampala School of Evangelical Theology by promising five days of weakness! One student commented that he had heard lots about power in the Christian life, but had never been shown that it was power to serve and to endure.

I think power to be weak can mean two things for us.

First, it means laying aside *our* power, our rights, our status. We become humble, lowly, meek, gentle. We become slaves, servants of God and servants of others. We no longer look to be served. Instead we look to serve and give our lives for others. We no longer jockey for privilege and status and influence. Instead we esteem others better than ourselves and put their interests above our own. This, as we saw in part two, is to follow the way of the cross.

Second, power to be weak means God uses our weakness, our frailty, our foolishness. He doesn't use superstars. He uses ordinary, weak, fragile people like you and me.

God uses people like Charlotte Elliot. She was known as 'carefree Charlotte' in her youth: beautiful, talented, at one point earning money as a comedy writer. But when she was thirty-two, she was struck down by a mystery illness that eventually left her paralysed and bedridden. She spent the next fifty years of her life in a daily round of pain and exhaustion.

One evening, visiting friends in London, Charlotte was asked by a Swiss evangelist, Cesar Malan, if she was a Christian. At the time, she took offence and said abruptly that she would rather not discuss the question. But then she couldn't shift it from her mind. Three weeks later, Charlotte saw Malan again and told him that, ever since their conversation, she'd been trying to find her Saviour. 'How can I come to Christ?' she asked. 'You have nothing of merit to bring to God. You must come, just as you are,' he replied.

Charlotte never recovered her health, but her heart was transformed. She once wrote:

> My Heavenly Father knows, and he alone, what it is, day after day, and hour after hour, to fight against bodily feelings of almost overpowering weakness and languor and exhaustion, to resolve,

> as he enables me to do, not to yield to the slothfulness, the depression, the irritability, such as this body causes me to long to indulge, but to rise every morning determined on taking this for my motto, 'If any man will come after me, let him deny himself, take up his cross daily, and follow me.'

She wrote over 150 songs, some of which were published as *The Invalid's Hymn Book*. Her most famous hymn echoes the words used to bring her to joy in Christ:

> Just as I am, without one plea,
> But that Thy blood was shed for me,
> And that Thou bidd'st me come to Thee,
> O Lamb of God, I come, I come.
>
> Just as I am, tho' tossed about
> With many a conflict, many a doubt,
> Fightings and fears within, without,
> O Lamb of God, I come, I come.

Referring to these words, her brother once said: 'In the course of a long ministry, I hope I have been permitted to see some of the fruit of my labour, but I feel that far more has been done by a single hymn of my sister's.' And that was before the hymn became the theme song of the campaigns by evangelist Billy Graham, so that weak, bedridden Charlotte was used by God to bring many thousands of people to share her joy in Christ.

The Lord 'said to me,' recalls Paul, '"My grace is sufficient for you, for my power is made perfect in weakness." Therefore I will boast all the more gladly about my weaknesses, so that Christ's power may rest on me' (2 Corinthians 12:9). He has been writing about a visionary ascent into heaven that was granted to him, but then reveals that along with it came an unspecified 'thorn in the flesh' – some kind of weakness (12:7). Paul learnt to boast in weakness because in weakness God's power is seen. Even the visionary *ascent* into heaven is mentioned by Paul alongside an ignominious *descent* from the wall of Damascus in a laundry basket (11:33)!

Where would you place yourself on a spectrum between power and weakness when you think about your involvement as a Christian in:

- the mission activities of your church?
- your workplace or school?
- your friends?
- other Christians?

power -- weakness

Are you towards the power end of the line or the weakness end? This is how Paul assessed his ministry:

> But we have this treasure in jars of clay to show that this all-surpassing power is from God and not from us. We are hard pressed on every side, but not crushed; perplexed, but not in despair; persecuted, but not abandoned; struck down, but not destroyed.
> (2 Corinthians 4:7–9)

Pressure, perplexity and persecution. Is that how the Christian life feels to you? Don't worry. Paul says there are good reasons why it's like that. Christians are the result of an act of new creation. Just as God said, 'Let light shine out of darkness' at the creation of the world, now again he speaks light into our dark hearts. He has given us 'the light of the knowledge of the glory of God in the face of Christ' (4:6). But we have this glory in 'jars of clay'. A typical household in Paul's time might have had a few metal containers for best, but day to day they used clay jars – easily broken, but cheap to replace. In God's household we're not golden vessels; we're clay pots. We have glory together with pressure, perplexity and persecution.

The great pioneer missionary, William Carey, established a printing workshop in Serampore, India, to translate and publish the Bible into new languages. In March 1812, while Carey was away, it burnt to the ground. Destroyed were a multi-language dictionary, two grammar books and whole, newly translated versions of the Bible. The following day a colleague broke the news to Carey. 'The work of years – gone in a moment,' Carey whispered in response. Yet soon after, he wrote: 'The loss is heavy, but as travelling a road the second time is usually done with greater ease and certainty than the first time, so I trust the work will lose nothing of real value. We are not discouraged; indeed the work is already begun again in every language. We are cast down, but not in despair.' And so Carey returned to the work. The news brought a wave of support from England and, twenty years on, Bibles, New Testaments or Bible books in forty-four languages and dialects had been produced from the replacement workshop.

This is the paradox of Christian ministry. A wonderful, glorious message through ordinary, plain, weak messengers. But any other way would only confuse the message. If my abilities were amazing, then people might look to me instead of God. If people found me impressive, they might think being a Christian was about being successful. But if I'm weak and faltering, then the focus will be where it belongs: on the power of God. Alister McGrath says: 'The full force of Paul's insights is missed if we interpret him as teaching that we can have life *despite* death and strength *despite* weakness: for Paul, the remarkable meaning of the enigma of the cross is that life comes *through* death and strength *through* weakness.'[57]

> When I came to you, brothers, I did not come with eloquence or superior wisdom as I proclaimed to you the testimony about God. For I resolved to know nothing while I was with you except Jesus Christ and him crucified. I came to you in weakness and fear, and with much trembling. My message and my preaching were not with wise and persuasive words, but with a demonstration of the Spirit's power, so that your faith might not rest on men's wisdom, but on God's power.
> (1 Corinthians 2:1–5)

Some people are immediately impressive, dynamic, persuasive, confident. Others flock to them. But they don't make good messengers of the cross. People want to be like the leader when their role model should be Christ. They feel confident when the leader is around when their trust should be in Christ. If the centre of our ministry is our wisdom, power or status, then we're sowing trouble. We'll produce people whose faith rests on human wisdom or power. But God will 'destroy the wisdom of the wise' (1:19).

The message and the messenger must match each other. It's possible to say one thing with our words and communicate another with our lives. We can talk about the foolishness and weakness of the cross, but live a message of power and success. Paul determined 'to know nothing while I was with you except Jesus Christ and him crucified'. He rejected eloquence and performance. As he proclaimed the message of Christ's service and sacrifice for us, so Paul himself modelled a life of service and sacrifice. 'It is not possible to proclaim the message of a Christ who was "crucified in weakness" in a triumphalist or overpowering manner. To do so would be to sell out to the ways of the world and build in a contradiction between the form and substance of the gospel.'[58] Pressure, perplexity and persecution aren't much fun! But they allow the message of God's power to shine through us and lead to gospel fruit and gospel glory.

Paul came to Corinth in weakness, proclaiming the weakness of the cross. What did he leave behind? A church. A church created not by his charisma or eloquence or arguments, but a church created by God's power (2:1–5).

Power in the church

As Christians, we often look to the world around us for leadership models. We read the latest management books, adapt the latest business theories, integrate the latest psychological models. Sometimes we do this explicitly, but often subconsciously. No doubt there's much wisdom out there. But Jesus emphasizes the fundamental difference between worldly leadership and Christian leadership. 'You know that those who are regarded as rulers of the Gentiles lord it over them, and their high officials exercise authority over them. Not so with you. Instead, whoever wants to become great among you must be your servant, and whoever wants to be first must be slave of all' (Mark 10:42–44). The cross redefines the nature of authority and leadership. Richard Mouw comments:

> The story of the reclamation of fallen humanity directly confronts the revisionist doctrine of God [put forward by the Serpent] that precipitated the fall into sin. Over and over, human beings must hear the refrain, 'You have misunderstood; that is not what it means to be a "lord".' Finally God himself must become a member of sinful humanity . . . The lie of the Tempter is

> decisively exposed when the incarnate Son says, 'Look! This is what it means to be a "lord"': and 'he emptied himself, taking the form of a servant . . . and became obedient unto death, even death on a cross' (Philippians 2:7–8).[59]

In 2 Corinthians 10 – 13, Paul takes on a group of church leaders who accused him of being timid and tame, while they were eloquent, dynamic and spiritual. We might expect Paul to assert his apostolic authority or point to his achievements. But then he would be employing the same boasting and power plays that he deplores in them! So he begins instead with 'the meekness and gentleness of Christ'. Paul's model is Christ, the King who exercised power through service and love. 'By the meekness and gentleness of Christ, I appeal to you – I, Paul, who am "timid" when face to face with you, but "bold" when away! I beg you that when I come I may not have to be as bold as I expect to be towards some people who think that we live by the standards of this world' (2 Corinthians 10:1–2).

Dynamism. Assertiveness. Eloquence. Power. Charisma. These are qualities we look for in leaders. These are what the leaders in Corinth valued. These are the standards of the world. Meekness and gentleness. This is the model of Christ. 'The weapons of the world' – rhetorical flourishes, spiritual pretensions and personal charisma – may gain a following, but they lack any power to bring obedience (10:3–6). Clearly, Paul does have authority from Christ, but his authority is 'for building you up rather than pulling you down' (10:8). His concern is not for his own status, but for the church's pure devotion to Christ (11:1–6). 'The theology of the cross insists that whatever power and authority is exercised over others, whether recognised or not, is power for others, rather than power over others.'[60]

Paul describes the troublemakers in Corinth as 'super-apostles' (11:5). He's being ironic. Those who serve with humility will be great in God's kingdom (Mark 9:33–35). The 'super-apostles' have turned it the other way round. They exalt themselves and so they deserve little respect.

This, sadly, is the world of much contemporary evangelicalism. We exalt the platform speakers who perform at Christian conferences. We prize the eloquence that Paul rejected (1 Corinthians 2:1–5). We value degrees whereas Jesus ignored his disciples' lack of education when choosing the twelve (Acts 4:13). We follow numerical success. We pursue career paths. Church leaders look like company directors. Conference speakers look like entertainers. We've taken the word 'minister' and somehow turned it into a designation of status, even though it actually means 'servant'. We reject the title 'Father' on the basis of Matthew 23:8–11, but adopt other status titles like 'Reverend' and 'Pastor'. Evelyn Ashley suggests that, while in the West we're not scandalized by the cross itself, we are scandalized by leadership modelled on the cross: 'leadership that displays human weakness, human limitation, human suffering, and human fragility, but functions in God's power'. 'Somewhere along the line, we seem to have fallen in the same trap as the Corinthian church. We have come to value power, control, and success.'[61]

We respect leaders with large congregations, big budgets and great platform performances. But Paul suggests we should respect those Christians who work hard, face danger and suffer for the gospel. So when Paul boasts, he points to his sufferings (11:23–29). 'If I must boast, I will boast of the things that show my weakness' (11:30; 12:5, 9). If refusing to push himself forward is weakness, then Paul will readily admit to being weak (11:20–21). For the 'super-apostles', ministry is about power, status and glory. For Paul, the cross defines

Christian service and that means sharing the weakness, sacrifice and shame of the cross. This is where God's wisdom, glory and power are revealed. And so these are the signs of true disciples and true leaders. Martin Luther said: 'Our Lord God fills his high office in an odd manner. He entrusts it to preachers, poor sinners, who tell and teach the message and yet live according to it only in weakness. Thus God's power always goes forward amid extreme weakness.'[62]

The 'super-apostles', in effect, were claiming that Paul was an inferior apostle and his followers were inferior Christians. And they were offering to 'super-charge' them. But 'superior' teaching leads to 'superior' Christians who look down on others. Christians – then and now – have their tribes with their tribal heroes (1 Corinthians 1:10–17). The result inevitably is 'quarrelling, jealousy, outbursts of anger, factions, slander, gossip, arrogance and disorder' (2 Corinthians 12:20). The gospel of Christ crucified levels us all. All that we are, we are through the grace of God. We have no basis for boasting – except in the cross (1 Corinthians 1:31).

Imagine the advert the 'super-apostles' might write for the position of church leader in Corinth:

Pastor wanted for a thriving, cosmopolitan congregation.
Must be:

- a dynamic personality
- an eloquent preacher with a theological degree
- highly spiritually gifted
- a strong, visionary leader

Attractive remuneration offered.

The disturbing thing is that this sounds like so many of the adverts that appear in Christian magazines today. What qualities would Paul look for? His ideal 'pastor' would be:

- a timid personality (though willing to take on the congregation)
- an uneducated and unimpressive preacher of Christ crucified
- loving, patient, kind, humble, gentle, forbearing
- a leader who is honest about his weaknesses[63]

Paul's conclusion is this: 'We are glad whenever we are weak but you are strong; and our prayer is for your perfection' (2 Corinthians 13:9). Paul is 'weak' = he wants to serve others in dependence upon God. The Corinthians are 'strong' = self-promoting and self-confident. Seen like this, it's little wonder that Paul prays for *their* perfection or, literally, their 'mending'. It's the same irony we see in 1 Corinthians 4:10–13:

> We are fools for Christ, but you are so wise in Christ! We are weak, but you are strong! You are honoured, we are dishonoured! To this very hour we go hungry and thirsty, we are in rags, we are brutally treated, we are homeless. We work hard with our own hands. When we are cursed, we bless; when we are persecuted, we endure it; when we are slandered, we answer kindly. Up to this moment we have become the scum of the earth, the refuse of the world.

15. FREEDOM TO SERVE, LIFE TO DIE

Freedom to serve

In Galatians 5:1, Paul says: 'It is for freedom that Christ has set us free. Stand firm, then, and do not let yourselves be burdened again by a yoke of slavery.' This is a great statement of Christian freedom, as is the whole of the letter of Galatians. Some people were claiming that Gentile believers needed to be circumcised in line with the law of Moses if they were going to be truly part of the church. Paul would have none of it. The logic of justification by faith alone is clear, he argues. We're saved completely through Christ's finished work without any additions on our part, and so, in the same way, we're part of God's people through Christ's finished work, without any additions on our part. Paul rejects completely any attempt to add stipulations. He refuses to countenance anything that might compromise our Christian freedom.

Paul won't compromise one inch of Christian freedom. And yet . . . And yet he goes on to say: 'You, my brothers, were called to be free. But do not use your freedom to indulge the sinful nature; rather, serve one another in love' (Galatians 5:13). Literally, what Paul is saying is that we are called to 'be *slaves* to one another'. Free to be slaves! Resurrection freedom is given, not that we might be served, but that we might serve.

Or consider Romans 6:18: 'You have been set free from sin and have become slaves to righteousness.' We've been set free. But that's not the end of the story. We've been set free that we might become slaves to righteousness. Free to be slaves!

Yet, strange as it may seem, this new slavery is true freedom. Freedom is not, as our culture often seems to suppose, having lots of choices. True freedom is the ability to be the best and do the best. Freedom for us human beings to be the people God intended us to be – imaging God, reflecting his glory, sharing his reign. God isn't a tyrant. That was the lie of the serpent in the Garden of Eden. God's reign is liberating. God is the master who brings true freedom.

Freedom is not, as our culture often seems to suppose, having lots of choices. True freedom is the ability to be the best and do the best.

Just as a fish is only free in water, so human beings are only truly free when they love God and others. A fish isn't imprisoned in the lake. It doesn't need to be set free from its watery confines. No, a fish is designed to flourish, to be free, to be a true fish *in water*. Anything else isn't freedom, but death. So it is with human beings. We're designed to flourish, to be free, to be truly human *under God's rule*. Anything else isn't freedom, but slavery and death.

One way that freedom becomes freedom to serve others

in love is in the case of those with a weak conscience. Meat offered for sale in the market of Corinth had probably been first offered to the gods in pagan temples. So some Christians felt they ought not to eat it. Paul argues that we're free either way. Idols are nothing since there's only one God, so it doesn't matter whether it's been offered to idols or not (1 Corinthians 8:4–6). 'Food does not bring us near to God; we are no worse if we do not eat, and no better if we do' (1 Corinthians 8:8). Here again, Paul is defending Christian freedom. But there's an important qualification: love trumps freedom.

> Be careful, however, that the exercise of your freedom does not become a stumbling-block to the weak. For if anyone with a weak conscience sees you who have this knowledge eating in an idol's temple, won't he be emboldened to eat what has been sacrificed to idols? So this weak brother, for whom Christ died, is destroyed by your knowledge. When you sin against your brothers in this way and wound their weak conscience, you sin against Christ. Therefore, if what I eat causes my brother to fall into sin, I will never eat meat again, so that I will not cause him to fall.
> (1 Corinthians 8:9–13)

'I will never eat meat again.' That's a radical curtailment of the freedom for which Paul has just been arguing! But love trumps freedom. What matters most is not my freedom, but my fellow Christian's spiritual well-being.

Paul applies the same principle to mission. 'Though I am free and belong to no man, I make myself a slave to everyone, to win as many as possible' (1 Corinthians 9:19). Paul is no longer under the Mosaic law (though he is under God's moral law). But to reach Jews he will live under the law (20). That's why, even though in Galatia Paul vehemently opposed Gentile circumcision because it threatened

Christian freedom, he himself had Timothy circumcised to facilitate mission to unbelieving Jews (Acts 16:3). Paul defends Christian freedom, but then uses that freedom to pursue whatever is best for mission.

'I am free and belong to no man.' It could be a slogan of our culture. 'You're not the boss of me.' 'You don't own me.' 'I did it my way.' The reality is that only those with the Spirit are truly free. And those indwelt by the Spirit don't stop with 'I am free and belong to no man.' We go on to say: 'I make myself a slave to everyone, to win as many as possible.'

C. T. Studd was as wealthy and successful as a young man might hope to be. He was educated at Eton College and Cambridge University. The captain of the university cricket team, he became known as England's most talented player. But then he experienced a profound spiritual renewal through the ministry of D. L. Moody. When he was twenty-five, he gave 90% of his inheritance away to the cause of mission. The remaining 10% he gave to his wife as a wedding gift. She promptly gave this remaining 10% away. Together they served as missionaries, part of the 'Cambridge Seven', a group of wealthy students who gave up their lives of privilege to proclaim Christ in China. After nearly ten years they returned home because of poor health. After a few years encouraging support for mission, Studd moved to India for six years before again returning with ill health. Yet even then he was not done, spending eighteen years in Congo. In my father's 1957 edition of his biography by Norman Grubb there is a photo of his boyhood home, a grand mansion – the sort of place that has various wings and classical columns. Inset is a small picture of a one-room wooden hut with rush roofing – Studd's home in Africa.

Michael Gorman detects in Paul's writing a common formula:[64]

Although [*status*], not [*selfishness*] but [*self-abasement/slavery*].

The formula is repeated throughout Paul's writing, to describe both Christ and those who would follow him. We see it classically in the hymn in Philippians 2:6–8:

Philippians 2:6–8

although status	[Christ Jesus] being in very nature God
not selfishness	did not consider equality with God something to be grasped
but self-abasement	but made himself nothing, taking the very nature of a servant . . .

But we see it repeated in Paul's own ministry and the pattern he commends to other Christians:

1 Corinthians 9:19

although status	though I am free and belong to no man
not selfishness	[implied in 9:12, 15, 18: 'I have not used any of these rights']
but self-abasement	I make myself a slave to everyone, to win as many as possible

1 Thessalonians 2:5–7

although status	as apostles of Christ we could have been a burden to you (6)
not selfishness	we never used flattery, nor did we put on a mask to cover up greed (5)
but self-abasement	but we were gentle among you, like a mother caring for her little children (7)

This pattern is a particular feature of 1 Corinthians. It recurs, not necessarily tightly in one verse, but as the structure of Paul's teaching on conflict, marriage, Christians with weaker consciences, the Lord's Supper, and the exercise of spiritual gifts. Throughout, the structure is the same: you are free in Christ [status], but don't use your freedom for selfish ends [not selfishness], but for serving others and building them up [but self-abasement / slavery]. For example, in 1 Corinthians 11 Paul argues: although social status gives some of you privileges at meals [status], don't humiliate those who have nothing [not selfishness], but wait for one another so you eat the Lord's Supper together in a worthy manner [but self-abasement / slavery]. In 1 Corinthians 12 – 14 he argues: although you have spiritual gifts [status], don't be inflated by your gifts or despise the gifts of others [not selfishness], but receive and use your gifts, both yours and others, for the common good [but self-abasement / slavery]. *Although status, not selfishness, but self-abasement.*

Most people would think Jane has every reason to take things easier, being in her seventies and walking with a stick. Yet Jane does not takes things easy, but opens her home to needy refugees.

Tref is shy and finds social situations hard-going. But he resists the temptation to hide in the kitchen, and instead makes the effort to talk to everyone.

Craig has had a great party invitation. But he honours his prior commitment to babysit for Dan and Angela.

Julia loves the theatre and ballet, but she goes to the pub quiz each week. It's not her scene, but she's committed to working with others to reach the people there for Christ.

Alfred loved the King James Version, old hymns and pews – they're what he'd known all his life. But he still supported change to reach a new generation with the gospel.

Matt's head spins every time he has to speak in public. But

every time, he contributes to the prayer meeting – even with a spinning head.

Sheila loves her home and she likes it tidy and ordered. But every week, she lets the youth club stomp all over it.

Kevin has a busy, demanding job as the CEO of a small firm. But every week, he finds time to have lunch with Mr Rogers, a housebound member of his church.

John Stott is one of the most influential Christian leaders of the twentieth century. His books have sold well over a million copies and he has spoken to large crowds all over the world. When I was a teenager I went to a conference where he was speaking. As people were gathering, my friend popped off to the toilet so I was left on my own, looking sheepish. An older man started talking to me, asking about what I was doing in life. I was relieved to have a friendly face to talk to. Then my friend returned and the man introduced himself: 'Hello, I'm John Stott.' My jaw hit the floor. John Stott was world famous and about to give the main address at the conference, but his concern was with the nerdy kid in the corner looking lonely. Since that day, I've probably read thirty or so of John Stott's books and heard him speak many times. But nothing has influenced me quite as much as that first encounter. That's the kind of leader I want to be. *Although status, not selfishness, but self-abasement.*

Ask yourself:

What freedoms do I forego to serve other Christians?

How am I adapting for the sake of mission?

To whom am I a slave so that I might win them?

Life to die

> Since, then, you have been raised with Christ, set your hearts on things above, where Christ is seated at the right hand of God. Set

> your minds on things above, not on earthly things. For you died, and your life is now hidden with Christ in God. When Christ, who is your life, appears, then you also will appear with him in glory.
>
> Put to death, therefore, whatever belongs to your earthly nature: sexual immorality, impurity, lust, evil desires and greed, which is idolatry.
>
> (Colossians 3:1–5)

In history, Christ's resurrection glory is hidden glory. The world doesn't see it. But one day it will be revealed when Christ appears in glory (4). It's the same for those who are in Christ. We have resurrection life, but it's a hidden life. 'Your life is now hidden with Christ in God' (3.) Look around the room the next time you meet with other Christians. Do you see people with resurrection life? With resurrection bodies, gloriously transformed and made new? Able to appear in locked rooms? With no signs of decay? Of course not. Our resurrection life is a hidden life. It will only be revealed when Christ is revealed (4). But it's real life and real power. Let's sum up:

- We have resurrection life.
- At present, it's a hidden life.
- One day it will be revealed in glory.

But there is one more statement to add:

- Resurrection life is revealed now in the way of the cross.

We can't see resurrection life and glory in our bodies because we don't yet have resurrection bodies. You can't spot it in people as they walk down the street. People with resurrection life and power don't glow in some special way! But you can spot it.

Colossians 3:5 gives us a clue. 'Put to death, therefore, whatever belongs to your earthly nature . . .' We've been given resurrection life *to put to death sin in our lives*. We have power for self-denial. We have life to die. '[Christ] died for all, that those who live should no longer live for themselves but for him who died for them and was raised again' (2 Corinthians 5:15). We no longer live for ourselves, but for Christ.

So you can see resurrection life in the way people live. You can spot it in their sacrificial love, their suffering for Christ, their submission to God, their self-denial. Our resurrection life is revealed now in our conformity to the way of the cross.

> We always carry around in our body the death of Jesus, so that the life of Jesus may also be revealed in our body. For we who are alive are always being given over to death for Jesus' sake, so that his life may be revealed in our mortal body.
> (2 Corinthians 4:10–11)

How is the 'the life of Jesus . . . revealed in our body'? As we 'carry around in our body the death of Jesus'. 'We always carry around in our body the death of Jesus' is another way of saying we deny ourselves and take up our cross. Our lives are patterned on the death of Jesus *through the life of Jesus*.

We have resurrection life to follow the way of the cross. We *need* resurrection life to follow the way of the cross. Denying ourselves, submitting to God's will, serving others with sacrificial love – all this is beyond us unless we have help from God! We're given the resurrection power of Jesus so that we might put into practice the cross of Jesus. We're given the resurrection life of Jesus so that we might live the death of Jesus.

16. THE SPIRIT OF RESURRECTION

The Spirit of resurrection

Asked what would be his priority if he returned to leadership in a local church, New Testament scholar Gordon Fee replied: 'No matter how long it might take, I would set about with a single passion to help a local body of believers recapture the New Testament church's understanding of itself as an eschatological community.'[65]

We've seen that there is, in the Christian life, a pattern of suffering followed by glory which reflects the cross and resurrection of Jesus. We've also seen how the experience of resurrection is not entirely future. We know *right now*, in the middle of history, resurrection power, freedom and life. The event of resurrection that every Jew expected would take place at the end of history has begun *in history*. It began in history because Jesus was raised in history as the foretaste and beginning of what's to come. And it began in history because Jesus sent his Spirit into the world. The Holy Spirit is the Spirit of the coming age, bringing the experience of resurrection into the present. The Spirit is the eschatological Spirit, making the life of the age to come a present reality in the Christian community.

In his sermon on the day of Pentecost, Peter identifies the coming of the Spirit as a fulfilment of Joel's prophecy about the last days. 'This is what was spoken by the prophet Joel: "In the last days, God says, I will pour out my Spirit on all people"' (Acts 2:16–17). The surprise was that this was taking place before the end of history. Eternal life, the life of the future age, is present in the middle of history through the Spirit (John 6:63; 7:38–39).

A seal

When you send children to school you put their name in their clothes. Otherwise they'll lose them. Paul says the Spirit is God's seal on us. He's God's nametag, making sure we're his until the day of glory. 'Having believed, you were marked in him with a seal, the promised Holy Spirit' (Ephesians 1:13; see also 2 Corinthians 1:22). Cattle and slaves were branded with a seal to show who was their owner and to protect them from theft. The Holy Spirit is God's mark of ownership on us. The seal of the Spirit is the sign that God will protect us as his own until the day of redemption (Ephesians 4:30). So the Spirit gives us that sense of confidence that we're part of God's family.

A guarantee

In Ephesians 1:14, Paul changes the metaphor from seal to guarantee: 'Having believed, you were marked in him with a seal, the promised Holy Spirit, who is a deposit guaranteeing our inheritance until the redemption of those who are God's possession – to the praise of his glory' (Ephesians 1:13–14).

The Spirit is God's guarantee that he will give us what he's promised to give us.

A deposit

This guarantee comes in the form of a deposit. If you pay a deposit for something, you get a slip of paper saying that it's yours. It can't be sold to anyone else. It guarantees that it belongs to you – even though you've not yet received it. The Holy Spirit is God's deposit to us. He's God's pledge that he'll deliver our glorious inheritance. God has made himself contractually obliged to complete his work of new creation and the Spirit is his signature on that contract. 'Now it is God who has made us for this very purpose and has given us the Spirit as a deposit, guaranteeing what is to come' (2 Corinthians 5:5; see also 1:20–22).

A foretaste

But the Spirit is more than a deposit and guarantee. Paul uses a word that also means a *first instalment*. The deposit has come in the form of a first instalment. When a man gives a woman an engagement ring, it's a pledge that he'll marry her. The Spirit is a pledge of our inheritance. But he's more than this. An engagement ring isn't a foretaste of marriage. But the Spirit gives us something of the reality of new creation in the present – even if it's only a fraction of what's to come. So the Spirit is more like a lover's kiss – both a pledge *and* a foretaste of married union. Or the gift of the Spirit is like being allowed into the kitchen to have a little taste of the wonderful banquet that's being prepared. The blessings of the Spirit are a foretaste of God's wonderful banquet. Through the Spirit, we already enjoy something of the life of the future in the Christian community.

Firstfruits

In Romans 8:23, Paul says we have 'the firstfruits of the Spirit'. This phrase recalls the Jewish festivals of Passover and Pentecost which celebrate God's goodness in both creation and redemption. At Passover the first barley crop was presented to God in gratitude for his provision. Fifty days later, at Pentecost, the first of the wheat harvest was presented. The firstfruits represented the greater harvest that was still to come. So when Paul describes the Spirit as the firstfruits, he's saying that the Spirit represents the greater harvest still to come. Passover also commemorated the liberation of God's people from slavery in Egypt and their escape from the angel of death through the blood of the Passover Lamb. This picture has been fulfilled in Jesus, the Lamb of God. The blood of Jesus redeems us from sin and death. The *greater* harvest still to come is the redemption of our bodies when we'll sin no more and no longer be subject to decay. In the meantime, the firstfruits of that harvest are our life in the Spirit. 'We ourselves, who have the firstfruits of the Spirit, groan inwardly as we wait eagerly for our adoption as sons, the redemption of our bodies' (Romans 8:23). We wait for our adoption as sons, but already we cry '*Abba*, Father'. How can we do this when our adoption is still future? Because we've 'received the Spirit of sonship' and 'the Spirit himself testifies with our spirit that we are God's children' (8:15–16).

The church is the community of the Holy Spirit (see 2 Corinthians 13:14). The Spirit creates in the life of the church a foretaste of the life of the new creation. We're the place where God lives by his Spirit (Ephesians 2:22) and where renewal is taking place through the Spirit (Titus 3:3–8). We're the place on earth where the future of the earth can be seen.

The empowering, liberating, life-giving Spirit

So when we speak of resurrection power, freedom and life, we're speaking of the work of the Spirit. He's the empowering Spirit who brings resurrection power; the liberating Spirit who brings resurrection freedom; and the life-giving Spirit who brings resurrection life. 'Through Christ Jesus the law of the Spirit of life set me free from the law of sin and death' (Romans 8:2; see also 8:10–11; 2 Corinthians 3:17). We're no longer under the tyranny of sin. We're no longer under the strictures of law. 'By dying to what once bound us, we have been released from the law so that we serve in the new way of the Spirit, and not in the old way of the written code' (Romans 7:6; Galatians 2:19). Instead we're led by the Spirit (Romans 8:14).

And along which road does the Spirit lead us?

The way of the cross in the power of the Spirit

Hebrews 9:14 says: 'How much more . . . will the blood of Christ, who through the eternal Spirit offered himself unblemished to God, cleanse our consciences from acts that lead to death, so that we may serve the living God!' At his baptism, the Spirit came upon Christ, empowering him for ministry. Here the writer of Hebrews suggests that this divine empowerment continues to the climax of Jesus' ministry, as he offers himself for his people. On the cross Jesus is abandoned by his Father, crying out, 'My God, my God, why have your forsaken me?' (Mark 15:34). But the Spirit is present with him, enabling him to offer himself to the Father. Even in death, Christ is not the victim of the Roman authorities, still less the passive victim of his Father. In the power of the Spirit, he is the agent of his own death, freely offering himself in love for his people (John 10:18).

The Spirit enabled Jesus freely to choose the cross. And

now, in the same way, the Spirit enables Christians to follow the way of the cross. The road along which the Spirit leads us is the Jerusalem road.

The Christian life is not a life of victory and power, nor is it a life of weakness. It's a life of power in weakness. Through the Holy Spirit we experience the power of resurrection from the coming age, so that we might follow the way of the cross in the present age. We must never separate the power of the resurrection from the way of the cross. We live in the power of the Spirit, but the Spirit-empowered life is characterized by service, love and submission. 'The distinctive feature of Paul's experience of the Spirit, and his resulting understanding of the essence of this Spirit, is the paradoxical symbiosis (union) of power and weakness, of power and cruciformity . . . Thus the criterion of the Spirit's activity is cruciformity, understood as Christ-like love in the edification of others rather than oneself.'[66]

We must never separate the power of the resurrection from the way of the cross.

This is how we steer between hopelessness on the one hand and triumphalism on the other. Triumphalism suggests we can experience now that which truly belongs to the renewal of creation. It trumpets 'victorious Christian living' in which stress is placed upon Christian victory and joy at the expense of the needs of the world and the ongoing power of sin in our lives. But discipleship now is always to follow the way of the cross and patiently to bear that cross, sustained by hope through the Spirit.

Yet the alternative to triumphalism is not hopelessness and inactivity. By the Holy Spirit, the power of the resurrection is at work in the life of the Christian community. The coming kingdom has already entered history through Christ the King, and his presence continues to be mediated by the Holy Spirit. The Spirit creates the life of the future kingdom now in the Christian community. We live in the power of the future through the Holy Spirit and in that power we serve the needs of the world.

We are people of power. We have power. We have resurrection power coursing through our bodies. God's mighty power, pulling Christ from the grave, is in your life.

But we don't have this power for victory over suffering, for an easy life, to lord it over others or to look down on unbelievers.

We have power to follow the way of the cross. To serve. To suffer. To love. To die.

We can do it. You can do it.

And as you do, you reveal Christ to people. 'We have this treasure in jars of clay to show that this all-surpassing power is from God and not from us' (2 Corinthians 4:7). You reveal Christ's transforming power to people. You reveal Christ's cross to people. You reveal Christ's grace to people.

One day the skies will be filled with the glory of God. One day everyone will see the resurrected glory of Jesus. He will blaze forth. Every knee will bow and every tongue confess that he is Lord, to the glory of God. One day.

But already his resurrection glory is being revealed. It's being revealed in your home. In your street. In your workplace. In your school. It's being revealed as you follow the way of the cross: as you deny yourself, as you serve others, as you love Jesus.

Part Five:
The promise of the resurrection – adventurous hope

We're looking forward to the renewal of creation and God's reign of life, love, justice and joy. This is a world worth living for and dying for. We live the way of the cross sustained by our hope of eternal glory. Our confident hope leads to a life of adventure and risk for Christ.

17. A RENEWED WORLD OF LIFE

How do you imagine life in the new heavens and the new earth?

The truth is that we don't really know what it will be like. That's because, whatever it's like strains our categories. It doesn't fit our language. How could God describe it to us? What images or words could he use that would mean anything to us? It would blow our time-bound imaginations.

But we're not left completely in the dark. We do know something about God's coming world.

From heaven to earth

For one thing, we know we won't be flitting around on the clouds. It won't be a ghostly, spiritual experience without bodies. We won't be in heaven – not for eternity. Or at least we won't be in heaven on its own. The Bible's vision of the future involves heaven being united with earth in a renewed creation.

The word 'heaven' is used a number of different ways in the Bible. It's used, for example, to describe the sky ('the heavens') together with the stars, moon and planets ('the heavenly bodies'). More commonly, heaven is used of a dimension woven into the fabric of the universe inhabited by spiritual beings. The heavenly realms are not a place above the sky (though the picture language of 'up' and 'down' is used). It's more like a 'space' within space. Two realms side by side in one universe. C. S Lewis captures this idea in his Narnia stories. There you can walk through a wardrobe or into a painting and find yourself in another world.

The heavenly realm intersects with our own when angels appear and demons possess. Jacob sees that intersection as a kind of portal in his dream of a stairway ascending up into heaven (Genesis 28:12). Stephen sees heaven opened as he's being martyred (Acts 7:55). The risen Jesus moves between these two dimensions. When he appears to his disciples in the locked room, I suspect he hasn't so much walked through a wall as moved between the heavenly and earthly realms (John 20:19).

The heavenly realms in this sense of the word are disputed territory. They're not a paradise, but a war zone. There're inhabited by good angels, but also by 'the spiritual forces of evil' who battle against us (Ephesians 6:12).

But the Bible also speaks of a battle in heaven which Satan has lost (Revelation 12). The death of Jesus on earth has won a victory in heaven. Christ now reigns over these spiritual forces (Ephesians 1:20) and shares the blessings of victory with his people (Ephesians 1:3; 2:6). At his ascension he moves from the earthly to the heavenly until the day he returns. In heaven he's enthroned and given 'all authority in heaven and on earth' (Matthew 28:18). His resurrected life is a heavenly life.

So 'heaven' is also used to describe the place where God is present and where his reign is acknowledged (Matthew 6:10). We're seated in heavenly places (Ephesians 2:6) and set our hearts on things above (Colossians 3:1–4), not because we'll live there eternally, but because this is where Christ is, and where Christ reigns, and from where Christ comes. Setting our hearts on things above doesn't mean dreaming of going to heaven. It means living for the new age that comes from heaven. We look to heaven because Christ is enthroned there and one day he will appear on earth.

Laying up treasure in heaven doesn't mean equipping a future home away from the earth. Because heaven is where God reigns now, it also represents the coming reality of his reign (Matthew 6:10). Laying up treasure in heaven means acting in ways that will bear fruit in eternity. When Peter talks about our inheritance being kept for us in heaven, we should think of treasure in a bank (1 Peter 1:4). The bank keeps it safe, but we don't go to the bank to enjoy it. One day God will take that treasure out of the bank so that we can enjoy it in his renewed earth. So heaven is 'the place where God's purposes for the future are stored up'.[67]

Philippi was a Roman colony. Its population had a strong sense of being citizens of Rome even though they didn't live there. This meant they lived in the style of Rome and recognized the authority of Rome. They saw themselves as an outpost of Roman civilization. Paul tells the Christians in Philippi that they're a colony of heaven. 'Our citizenship is in heaven. And we eagerly await a Saviour from there, the Lord Jesus Christ, who, by the power that enables him to bring everything under his control, will transform our lowly bodies so that they will be like his glorious body' (Philippians 3:20–21). Our spirits pass into the heavenly realm and the presence of Jesus when we die. But our ultimate future is a new heaven and new earth. We're not waiting to *go to* heaven. We're waiting for our Saviour to *come from* heaven. One day our King will come to earth and the court of heaven will be set up in the territory of earth. 'The force of Philippians 3:20 is not, as has often been thought, that heaven as such is the homeland of Christians to which they, as perpetual foreigners on earth, must strive to return, but rather that since our Lord is in heaven their life is to be governed by the heavenly commonwealth and this realm is to be determinative for all aspects of their life.'[68] We're citizens of heaven because we live in the style of heaven and recognize the authority of the King enthroned in heaven. We live as an outpost of heavenly civilization.

A renewed world

Christians don't emphasize the immortality of the soul. The Bible instead affirms the resurrection of the body. We won't spend eternity in a disembodied state communing through some kind of telepathy. We'll be living with physical bodies in a physical world, albeit new resurrection bodies in a new, recreated world. Commenting on Romans 8:18–23, Martyn Lloyd-Jones says:

> As I understand it, what is commonly described as 'heaven' in the Scripture is what we should regard as the intermediate state, not the final state, not the eternal state . . . Our eternal state is not going to be lived in the heavens, in the air, in some vague, nebulous spiritual condition . . . Heaven in an eternal sense is going to be 'heaven on earth'. Heaven on earth – that is where we shall spend eternity, and not as disembodied spirits, for the whole man shall be redeemed, the body included. A concrete body must have a concrete world . . . You and I, the redeemed, will dwell in our glorified bodies on a glorified earth under the glorified heavens.[69]

Creation and eschatology go together in this respect. Eschatology is, if you like, the doctrine of *re*-creation. The Christian doctrine of creation maintains that the world God created was a good world. The physical and bodily are not lesser than the spiritual and mental. The Christian doctrine of the future maintains that the world God created will again be a good world when he recreates it. The old creation is not thrown in the dustbin, but purified and renewed. God's purposes in creation are not thwarted by sin or destroyed at the end of time. They're fulfilled in the new creation.

The proof of this is the resurrection of Jesus. The resurrection is the demonstration of God's eschatological intentions. Christ is the 'firstborn from among the dead' (Colossians 1:18). He's the pattern for all his people: the new Adam (1 Corinthians 15:20–23). And Christ rose with a physical body. It could be touched. He walked and ate with his disciples. It was a transformed body, but it was clearly a physical body.

A reunited world

At the end of history, heaven will be united with earth. Christians don't go *up* to heaven. John sees the heavenly Jerusalem 'coming *down* out of heaven from God, prepared as a bride beautifully dressed for her husband' (Revelation 21:2). The heavenly presence of God comes *to earth*. 'And I heard a loud voice from the throne saying, "Now the dwelling of God is with men, and he will live with them. They will be his people, and God himself will be with them and be their God"' (Revelation 21:3). God is now among his people and 'the earth will be filled with the knowledge of the glory of the LORD, as the waters cover the sea' (Habakkuk 2:14).

In history, the rebellion against God has spilt backwards and forwards between the earthly and heavenly realms. Christians on earth battle against 'spiritual forces of evil in the heavenly realms'. Unseen by us, angels war against the forces of Satan (Daniel 10:13; Revelation 12:7). But there at the centre of heaven is the victorious Lamb of God. The battle is won. His death spans heaven and earth. His death restores harmony to the entire cosmos, both heaven and earth. 'For God was pleased to have all his fulness dwell in him, and through him to reconcile to himself all things, whether things on earth or things in heaven, by making peace through his blood, shed on the cross' (Colossians 1:19–20). The future for heaven and the future for earth is finally to be brought together in Christ, through Christ and under Christ. 'And he made known to us the mystery of his will according to his good pleasure, which he purposed in Christ, to be put into effect when the times will have reached their fulfilment – to bring all things in heaven and on earth together under one head, even Christ' (Ephesians 1:9–10).

A world of life

Death isn't natural. It's not part of the world God made. It's an intrusion. A scar on creation. We'd rather not talk about it, but its shadow lies across our lives. We fear death. The symptoms of this fear are all around us: hypochondria, the fetish for fitness, plastic surgery and other attempts to remain looking young, midlife crises when we realize our lives are slipping away. People live in denial of death by filling their lives with other things. They create substitutes for their failing youth: fast cars, younger partners, anything that will create the illusion of power and performance. We even lie about our age so we can at least pretend death is far away.

But the resurrection of Christ is the defeat of death for all who are in Christ.

> When the perishable has been clothed with the imperishable, and the mortal with immortality, then the saying that is written will come true: 'Death has been swallowed up in victory.'
>
> 'Where, O death, is your victory?
> Where, O death, is your sting?'
>
> The sting of death is sin, and the power of sin is the law. But thanks be to God! He gives us the victory through our Lord Jesus Christ.
>
> (1 Corinthians 15:54–57)

The resurrection of Jesus is the beginning of eternal life.

The resurrection of Jesus is the beginning of eternal life. Jesus is 'the firstborn among many brothers' (Romans 8:29; 1 Corinthians 15:20). Death has given way to life. And Christ's life is the promise of life after death to all who believe.

The resurrected body of Jesus was both *like* his pre-death body (it still bore the nail marks) and *unlike* his pre-death body (he appeared in locked rooms). So it will be with the totality of God's new creation. It will be this earth, but transformed, renewed and purged from sin. Like this earth and unlike this earth. Paul uses the analogy of seeds to described the relationship between our current bodies and our resurrection bodies (1 Corinthians 15:35–44). Apple seeds produce apple trees. They don't turn into something else. There is continuity. But apple trees are very different to apple seeds. Jesus, says Tom Wright, 'is still human, still in fact an *embodied* human – actually, a *more solidly embodied* human that we are'.[70] Paul contrasts our current natural bodies with our future spiritual bodies (1 Corinthians 15:35–50). We mustn't think of spiritual bodies as non-physical bodies (whatever that might mean). Tom Wright explains the word 'spiritual' like this:

> Adjectives of this type, Greek adjectives ending in *–ikos*, do not describe the material out of which things are made, but the power or energy which animates them. It is the difference between asking on the one hand 'is this a wooden ship or an iron ship?' (the material from which it is made) and asking on the other 'is this a steam ship or a sailing ship?' (the energy which empowers it). Paul is talking about the present body, which is animated by the normal human *psychē* (the life-force we all possess here and now, which gets us through the present life but is ultimately powerless against illness, injury, decay and death), and the future body which is animated by God's *pneuma*, God's breath of new life, the energizing power of God's new creation.[71]

The miracles of Jesus are sometimes described in the Gospels using the Greek word for 'to save' (it usually gets translated as 'healed'). This doesn't just mean his miracles were physical pictures of a spiritual reality. Nor does it mean that every Christian can expect Jesus to heal them from every illness. It means the miracles of Jesus were a foretaste of the physical renewal in the new creation. They were a sign, a beginning, a taster, a demonstration of what God will do at the end of time. For a moment in history, Jesus fed the poor. At the end of time, all God's people will join his messianic banquet. For a moment in history, Jesus healed the sick. At the end of time, God will heal all our infirmities. For a moment in history, Jesus cast out demons. At the end of time, God will defeat Satan forever. For a moment in history, Jesus raised the dead. At the end of time, God will raise the dead and death will be no more. We can't conceive what the new creation will be like. But the Bible often describes it in terms of what it's *not* like. 'There will be no more death or mourning or crying or pain, for the old order of things has passed away' (Revelation 21:4).

Death abounds in our world. But life will abound in God's coming world.

18. A WORLD OF JUSTICE, JOY AND LOVE

The film *Arlington Road* is the story of a man called Michael Faraday, a widower whose wife was an FBI agent killed in action. Faraday begins to suspect that his neighbour, Oliver Lang, is planning a terrorist attack on a federal building. Faraday's new girlfriend leaves because she thinks he's paranoid. His son is antagonized when Faraday tries to stop him mixing with Lang's family.

Finally, Faraday gets the evidence he needs, but not before they've kidnapped his son. Seeing his son in the back of a van, he trails it to the terrorists' base. He struggles with Lang before rushing back to his car to find the van gone. He pursues it, following it into the FBI building. FBI agents surround him, trying to restrain him. He's frantic, shouting that there's a bomb in the van. But when the van is opened, it's empty. And then the action goes into slow motion as he realizes that, while he was struggling with Lang, the terrorists switched the bomb into the car he drove into the building. As he opens the boot, the bomb explodes.

The film moves on to a series of news reports showing the carnage and placing the blame on Faraday himself. The movie closes with his son looking distraught, trying to come to terms with his belief that his father is a murderer. Meanwhile Lang and wife, calm as you like, wait for their next assignment.

It's a very disturbing film. All the time, you hope – you expect – that Faraday will expose the terrorists, get there in time, rescue his son, prevent tragedy. But that's not how it ends. The good guy loses. He gets the blame. This offends our sense of justice. We long for another ending. We long for justice. But the credits roll. This is how it is. Evil triumphs.

A world of justice

We long for justice. Deep inside, we want right to be rewarded and evil to be punished. That's why crowds of people gather outside court buildings when notorious criminals are on trial. When I heard that General Pinochet, the former dictator in Chile, had been arrested, I involuntarily cheered. I couldn't help myself.

In Ecclesiastes the writer concludes that everything is meaningless. Even trying to be righteous is meaningless because the righteous end up no better off than the wicked (Ecclesiastes 8:14). If you exclude God from the picture – if you look at life 'under the sun' – everything is meaningless (1:14). But the book ends: 'God will bring every deed into judgment, including every hidden thing, whether it is good or evil' (12:14). In a world without judgment, everything is meaningless. Good is no different from evil. There's no basis for calling something 'right' and something else 'wrong'.

But God will reorder the world. God will impose order and meaning through judgment.

At one point in the television series *World at War*, a man, a Christian as it happens, sees a railway truck full of people. They're Jews being transported to a concentration camp. He sees they're desperate for a drink, so he starts handing cups of water up to them. He doesn't know exactly what's happening, but he realizes it isn't good. Eventually he's seen by a guard who pushes him away. As he's pushed away, he says, 'You will not get away with this.' It wasn't a statement of faith in the victory of the allies. It was a statement of faith – even of hope – in God. One day God will call us to account.

The Bible promises a day of reversal when the first shall be last and the last shall be first. The verdict of the world will be overturned. The court of final appeal will be held. The wicked will be judged and the righteous will be vindicated. The resurrection of Jesus was the ultimate reversal. Jesus is condemned by humanity as a blasphemer and a troublemaker. But God overturns the verdict of the cross when he raises Christ to life. The resurrection is the sign that justice will triumph. God's rule will one day be reasserted over his world and his rule is a rule of justice.

That's why the kingdom of God is good news to the poor. The reign of Jesus will be a reign of justice.

> He will judge your people in righteousness,
> your afflicted ones with justice.
> The mountains will bring prosperity to the people,
> the hills the fruit of righteousness.
> He will defend the afflicted among the people
> and save the children of the needy;
> he will crush the oppressor.
> (Psalm 72:2–4)

He will reign on David's throne
  and over his kingdom,
establishing and upholding it
  with justice and righteousness
  from that time on and for ever.
(Isaiah 9:7)

He will not judge by what he sees with his eyes,
  or decide by what he hears with his ears;
but with righteousness he will judge the needy,
  with justice he will give decisions for the poor of the
    earth.
(Isaiah 11:3–4)

Here at last will be a kingdom of justice. Here is a land where there are no victims of crime, no drug addicts, where there is no debt, no homelessness. Where parents don't bury their children and widows don't weep over their husbands' graves. Where swords are beaten into ploughshares and spears into pruning hooks. Where no-one is deceived, no-one is threatened, no-one is lonely. God's kingdom is good news to the victims of injustice.

The problem with this coming world of justice is that, while many of us are victims of injustice, none of us is just. It's all well and good to cry out for justice, but none of us has always done right by other people. And none of us has done right by God.

The good news is that we're justified – declared just – by the death and resurrection of Jesus. God's people are declared just (even though we're unjust) and God is just in declaring us just (even though we're unjust) because on the cross Jesus himself experienced the judgment of God in our place. So the resurrection which vindicates Christ also vindicates those who are in Christ. 'He was delivered over to death for our sins and was raised to life for our justification' (Romans 4:25). God's kingdom is a kingdom of justice because it's founded on the cross and resurrection.

Injustice and oppression abound in our world. But justice and peace will abound in God's coming world.

A world of joy

Every longing in us is a version of our longing for God. That longing may be a distorted version of our longing for God, but it's still a longing for the God we were made to know. C. S. Lewis says: 'There have been times when I think we do not desire heaven; but more often I find myself wondering whether, in our hearts of hearts, we have ever desired anything else . . . It is the secret signature of each soul, the incommunicable and unappeasable want.'[72] Augustine famously said, 'Our hearts are restless till they find their rest in you.' In the new creation, our hearts fully and finally find their rest in God. Our restless striving for more gives way to an eternal rest in God. G. K. Chesterton says:

> A man varies his movements because of some slight element of failure or fatigue. He gets into a bus because he is tired of walking; or he walks because he is tired of sitting still. But if his life and joy were so gigantic that he never tired of going to Islington, he might go to Islington as regularly as the Thames goes to Sheerness . . . His routine might be due, not to a lifelessness, but to a rush of life. The thing I mean can be seen, for instance, in children, when they find some game or joke that they specially enjoy. A child kicks his legs rhythmically through excess, not absence, of life. Because children have abounding vitality, because they are in spirit fierce and free, therefore they want things repeated and unchanged. They always say,

> 'Do it again'; and the grown-up person does it again until he is nearly dead. For grown-up people are not strong enough to exult in monotony. But perhaps God is strong enough to exult in monotony. It is possible that God says every morning, 'Do it again' to the sun; and every evening, 'Do it again' to the moon. It may not be automatic necessity that makes all daisies alike; it may be that God makes every daisy separately, but has never got tired of making them. It may be that He has the eternal appetite of infancy; for we have sinned and grown old, and our Father is younger than we. The repetition in Nature may not be a mere recurrence; it may be a theatrical encore.[73]

We're so easily bored with life. The things that bring us pleasure soon lose their appeal. We become experience-junkies in constant pursuit of something to entertain us. No wonder we often think that life in the new creation will be boring. But God is never bored. His joy and life are so gigantic that he never loses interest in sunrises and daisies. They are ever new, ever fresh, ever fun.

Sadness abounds in our world. But joy will abound in God's coming world.

A world of love

In a famous sermon, the American preacher and theologian Jonathan Edwards described heaven as 'a world of love'.[74] He based his sermon on 1 Corinthians 13:8. The gifts of prophecy and tongues will cease, but 'love never fails'. He wrote:

> Oh, what joy there will be springing up in our hearts when, after our weary pilgrimage, we are brought to a paradise like this! Here is joy unspeakable, full of glory. Here is joy that is humble, holy, captivating, and divine in its perfection!
>
> Love is always a sweet thing, especially divine love. Even on

earth, love is a spring of sweetness. But in heaven it will become a stream, a river, an ocean! All shall stand around the God of glory, who is the great fountain of love. We will open our very souls to be filled with the love that pours out from his fullness.

We will be like flowers in the bright and joyous days of spring, opening their petals to be filled with the light and warmth of the sun, flourishing in beauty and fragrance under its cheering rays. Every saint in heaven is like a flower in the garden of God. And holy love is the sweet fragrance they all send forth, filling paradise with its scent.

Every soul there is like a note in some concert of delightful music, beautifully harmonizing with every other note, so that together they blend into the most rapturous song, praising God and the Lamb forever.

And so everyone helps each other to express to their fullest capacity the love of the whole community to its glorious Father and Head. Together they pour back love into the great fountain of love from which they are supplied and filled with love, and blessing, and glory.

And so they will love, and reign in love, and share the godlike joy that is its fruit in a way that no eye has seen, no ear has heard, no mind has ever imagined. In the full sunlight of the throne, captivated with joys that are forever increasing and yet forever full, they shall live and reign with God and Christ forever and ever![75]

Hatred abounds in our world. But love will abound in God's coming world.

19. A WORLD WORTH LIVING FOR AND A WORLD WORTH DYING FOR

Treasure in heaven

Jesus says: 'Do not store up for yourselves treasures on earth, where moth and rust destroy, and where thieves break in and steal. But store up for yourselves treasures in heaven, where moth and rust do not destroy, and where thieves do not break in and steal' (Matthew 6:19–20)

The tragedy is that most people are living for treasure on earth. Even many Christians live for the things of this passing age. And it is a tragedy. A waste. Wealth doesn't satisfy. Adverts promise satisfaction, but in fact they are designed to create dissatisfaction. Wealth corrodes. It's fragile. Fleeting. 'Moth and rust destroy, and . . . thieves break in and steal.' It's like sand slipping through our fingers.

We're pilgrims in this world. Refugees. Strangers. (See Hebrews 11:13–16; 1 Peter 2:11.) This world as it is now is not our home. We pass through life looking ahead to something bigger and better. One day this earth will be a 'home of righteousness' (2 Peter 3:13), but only when we arrive at a heavenly version of this earth. Only when this earth comes under a new regime. Only when Christ is at the centre and his glory fills the horizons.

There's a lot of talk today about 'faith journeys'. The language sounds very much like John Bunyan's famous allegorical story, *Pilgrim's Progress*. But there's a crucial difference. Pilgrim's journey, as for all true Christians, was a journey between two fixed points: between death and life; between the cross and resurrection. Modern faith journeys are very different. They're explorations without a clear beginning and without a clear destination. Who knows where they might end? They're journeys *from* home, not *to* home. Pilgrim's journey starts at the cross when the burden of his sins rolls away and then he heads out in a specific destination – the celestial city.

The Bible often talks about future reward. Some Christians feel uneasy about this. Does it mean we serve God for selfish reasons? The answer is that we need to realize that future rewards are intrinsic to our service – they're its fulfilment, its outflow, its climax. It's not like giving sweets to a child for practising the piano. It's more like the joy of being able to play beautiful music. It's not a bribe, but the pleasure of fulfilment. It's the pleasure of seeing how our service has contributed to God's glory. It's hearing the words: 'Well done, good and faithful servant!' (see Matthew 25:23). 'Delight yourself in the LORD and he will give you the desires of your heart' (Psalm 37:4). If we treasure Christ, then he himself will be our reward.

The call of Jesus to lay up treasure in heaven poses several questions to us.

1. Where is your treasure?

What's the thing you value most? What gives you more pleasure than anything else? Jesus says, 'Where your treasure is, there your heart will be also' (Matthew 6:21). Where's your heart? What do you treasure? How would you complete the sentence: 'I'd be really happy if . . .' What really matters to you? Our actions always show what we really treasure or value.

Why don't we live below the average income and give the rest to the poor? Why don't we move into needy neighbourhoods? Why don't we open our homes to hurting people? Why don't we work four days a week to create more time for mission? Why don't we take low-paid jobs to serve the community? We have some very sophisticated reasons. I know because I use them. But most of the time, it comes down to this: our treasure is earthly treasure and our security is earthly security.

2. *What are you looking at?*

'The eye is the lamp of the body. If your eyes are good, your whole body will be full of light. But if your eyes are bad, your whole body will be full of darkness. If then the light within you is darkness, how great is that darkness!' (22–23). Look to the light and you can navigate properly. But look at what is false or dark and your life will be full of confusion. Imagine walking across a field. If you fix your eyes on the gate you're heading towards, then you'll walk in a straight line across the field. But if you constantly look away to the left, you'll veer off course.

So what are you looking at? If you want to keep on the right path in life, then you must keep looking ahead, keep meditating on the future life. If, however, you focus your attention on your worries or other people's possessions or a thousand adverts or uncritical television watching, then don't be surprised if you wander off course. 'Sometimes people ask us if we are scared, living in the inner city,' say Shane Claiborne and Jonathan Wilson-Hartgrove. 'We usually reply with something like, "We're more afraid of shopping malls." The Scriptures say we should not fear those things which can destroy the body, but we are to fear that which can destroy the soul (Matthew 10:28).'[76]

3. *Whom are you serving?*

Whatever you value most will inevitably be what you end up serving. Of course it will, because that's what matters most to you: what you plan for, what you act for, what you worry about. Here's the vicious cycle of greed:

look at possessions ➪ treasure possessions ➪ serve possessions ➪ hate God

Yes, serving wealth will make you hate God! 'No-one can serve two masters,' says Jesus. 'Either he will hate the one and love the other, or he will be devoted to the one and despise the other. You cannot serve both God and Money' (24). It's a very sober statement. If your priority is earthly treasure, then God will become an unwelcome distraction. But you can break the cycle:

look at God revealed in Christ ➪ treasure God ➪ serve God ➪ love God

Paul Tripp says: 'Jesus demands everything, not just so we would submit to his control, but to free us from the control of things that were never designed to control us.'[77]

4. *What dominates your thoughts?*

Four times in Matthew 6, Jesus says: 'Do not worry' (25, 28, 31, 34). Worry is letting food and clothing dominate your thoughts. What should dominate our thoughts is God's kingdom (33).

Here's a tip: Your thoughts will follow your money. 'For where your treasure is, there your heart will be also' (21). So we can use our giving to retrain our desires and interests. Spend money on things and those things will matter to you. I remember seeing a beautiful, new car parked on our street and thinking, 'Wouldn't it be lovely to have a car like that?' And then I thought, 'No! I'd only worry about it getting scratched.' So use money to retrain your desires and interests by giving it away. Spend money on mission and other people, and mission and other people will become what interests you.

Living in eternity

I have a friend who lives entirely in the moment. He never thinks of consequences. It's wreaked havoc in his life. He's lost jobs and homes because he did what brought him pleasure in the moment, even if that meant skipping work or rent. But I'm also aware that middle-class people, like me, constantly plan for the future. We live in tomorrow. As a result we're not free to seek first God's kingdom today. We're not free to be generous with our time or money or work. Jesus says: 'Therefore do not worry about tomorrow, for tomorrow will worry about itself. Each day has enough trouble of its own' (34). Worry is living in tomorrow.

What we should be doing is not living for today (like my friend), nor for tomorrow (like me), but living for eternity. 'Do not store up for yourselves treasures on earth . . . store up for yourselves treasures in heaven' (19–20).

What we should be doing is not living for today (like my friend), nor for tomorrow (like me), but living for eternity.

Every day, we're making sacrifices. We study hard, work hard, exercise hard. We put up with annoying people. We skimp and save. We make sacrifices to gain something better. It's a principle we all accept and by which we all live. The question is: is what you're sacrificing for really worth it?

Long hours at the office. What do they bring? Wealth. Reputation. Security. Is it worth it?

Long hours partying. What do they bring? Friends. Pleasure. Fun. Is it worth it?

Long hours working on your home. What do they bring? Comfort. Style. Status. Is it worth it?

From the perspective of today, they might seem worthwhile. But from the perspective of eternity? At best, these things will last a lifetime. At best.

Long hours serving Christ. What do they bring? Eternal joy. Eternal love. Eternal honour. Is it worth it? Judge for yourself!

Francis Schaeffer preached a famous sermon which was subsequently published as an essay entitled 'Ash Heap Lives'.[78] 'We all tend to live "ash heap lives",' he explains. 'We spend most of our time and money for things that will end up in the city dump.' The central image was suggested by a boyhood experience:

> Have you ever walked through a city dump? You should. When I was growing up in Philadelphia, I would hike every Saturday. To get to the clean air of the country, I used to save a couple miles by tramping through the city dump. I have never forgotten this. It was a place of junk, fire, stench. It has helped me tremendously to think back on that place, because even as a boy I realized that I saw there almost everything people spend their money for. That was where their investment ended.

Here are some extracts from that powerful sermon:

> A man is a fool to put money in a bank that is not going to last when he can deposit it in a bank that will . . . Death is a thief. Five minutes after we die, our most treasured possessions which are invested in this life are absolutely robbed from us. . . .
>
> Let me say with tears that as far as material possessions, time, energy and talents are concerned, all too many Bible-believing Christians live as though their entire existence is limited to this side of the grave. We cannot ignore Jesus' statement about these two irreconcilable reference points: 'You cannot serve God and money.' (Matt. 6:24) Either riches in this life, or the reality of God and the future – one of them must give the overshadowing cast to our lives. To the extent that wealth (or power) is our reference point, we are spiritually poor . . . We cannot expect the power of God if our reference point is the things of this world, for practical materialism and true spirituality have no affinity for one another . . .
>
> In our culture nothing has exhibited such folly more than our automobiles. Go to a showroom and see the pride with which a man drives out his new car. Then think of an automobile graveyard or a rusting, stripped, junked car, abandoned on a city street. They are shells screaming out tremendous sermons against all practical materialism: 'You're fools! You're fools! You're fools!' And Christians – as well as any others – can be such fools with their wealth.

Someone mentioned on the phone to me recently the death from cancer of a prominent Christian leader in his fifties. She described it as a tragedy. But his death wasn't a tragedy. It was certainly a loss to his family, friends and to the wider church. But it is wasn't a tragedy. It was gain. Let me tell you what *is* a tragedy: Someone who gets a good education, secures a well-paid job, buys a house in a nice area, marries and has children, and ensures his children get a good education, so the cycle can begin again. Someone who treats Christ as a hobby or an insurance against hell. Someone who leaves behind a rusting car and children who've been trained to be self-indulgent. Someone with no gospel legacy. That's the tragedy.

Friends on the other side

In Luke 16, Jesus tells the story of an estate manager who realizes he'll soon be sacked for wasting his employer's money. So he uses what time he has left to cancel the debts people owe to his master in the hope that in turn they'll help him when he's out of work. Perhaps to our surprise, Jesus commends his actions, saying: 'I tell you, use worldly wealth to gain friends for yourselves, so that when it is gone, you will be welcomed into eternal dwellings' (Luke 16:9). Schaeffer comments:

> If you are a Christian, you are really going to be in Heaven, and some of the people you now know will be there, and they will speak with you about what you did in this life. Somebody will say to you, 'Thank you so much for the money you gave me when my children were starving. I didn't have a chance to thank you then, but I do now.' 'I remember the night you opened your home to me, when you moved over and shared your table with me.' This is what Jesus was saying, and He implied that you are a fool if you do not keep this in mind.

In the film *Big Fish*, Edward Bloom has been telling tales all his life. So much so that his son, Will, feels he doesn't know his father at all. Edward Bloom is now dying and Will comes home for his final days. As the tales are told again, bit by bit Will comes to realize that behind each story is some element of truth. At the end of the film, Edward suffers a stroke that leaves him unable to speak. It falls to Will to tell the final tale. He rushes his father out of the hospital and down to the riverside where all the characters that have populated Edward's stories are gathered: the friends he's made along the way, the people he's helped, a giant, a circus ringmaster, a werewolf, conjoined dancers. They shake hands, laugh, express their gratitude, before Edward, turning into a big fish, is released by Will into the river. His friends have gathered to see him off – as they do in real life a few days later at his funeral where the stories are again retold.

And so it is for Christians. Except that our friends won't gather on this side of the river; they'll gather on Jordan's farther bank. They won't see us off as we leave this life; they'll welcome us as we arrive in the next life.

Wealth you can take with you

I love going to the British Museum. You can reach out to touch things from Bible times – or at least you could if they weren't protected in glass cases. It feels a little like the Bible story is there before you. You can see papyri from New Testament times, statues from Assyria and golden sarcophagi from ancient Egypt.

We know from the pyramids and the sphinxes that the Egyptian rulers were very wealthy. They had the equivalent of today's multi-millionaire lifestyles. And Moses had it all. He was a child of the royal court. He could have anything and do anything. But he gave it all up because he was looking ahead. He wasn't living for this life.

> By faith Moses, when he had grown up, refused to be known as the son of Pharaoh's daughter. He chose to be ill-treated along with the people of God rather than to enjoy the pleasures of sin for a short time. He regarded disgrace for the sake of Christ as of greater value than the treasures of Egypt, because he was looking ahead to his reward. (Hebrews 11:24–26)

The Egyptians locked up their treasures in the pyramids so that they could take them into the afterlife. But they couldn't. How do I know? Because I've seen their treasures in the British Museum. Moses, though, still has his reward.

'You can't take it with you,' people say. Not true. You *can* take it with you. But first you must convert it into the currency of heaven and that currency is love and good works. You take it with you by giving it away!

> Command those who are rich in this present world not to be arrogant nor to put their hope in wealth, which is so uncertain, but to put their hope in God, who richly provides us with everything for our enjoyment. Command them to do good, to be rich in good deeds, and to be generous and willing to share. In this way they will lay up treasure for themselves as a firm foundation for the coming age, so that they may take hold of the life that is truly life. (1 Timothy 6:17–19)

How do we lay up treasure in heaven? By being generous with earthly treasure.

'They're too heavenly minded to be any earthly use,' people say. Not true. In fact, it's the other way round. You'll be no earthly use until you're heavenly minded. It's not those whose affections are rooted in this earth who exercise love for others to the full. They're too busy running after the things of this age (Matthew 6:31–32). Too worried about tomorrow to give generously today. It's those whose hearts are set on things above who are truly free to put God's kingdom first. Only those unconcerned about earthly treasure will be generous with that treasure.

Without Christian hope, we are left with a limp Christianity in which immediate experience is everything. That may be a charismatic experience with highs and healing. It may be a conservative experience of freedom from guilt and reassuring orthodoxy. It may be a pietistic experience with leadings from God and peace in my heart. But they all lack the rigour to meet the demands of the way of the cross. What sort of faith arises from hope? 'It is,' says Calvin, 'an earnest faith, full of power, so that it shirks no task when our neighbours are in need of help.'[79]

- What did you do yesterday for your present comfort or security? What did you do yesterday for God's future?
- What did you do last week because you saw an advert or you saw something someone else had? What did you do last week because of your confidence in God's promises?
- What will you do tomorrow to store up treasure on earth? What will you do tomorrow to store up treasure in heaven?
- When did you last take a risk for God? What did you risk?
- Hebrews 11:25 says the pleasures of sin last only for a short time. Psalm 16:11 says that at God's right hand 'are eternal pleasures'. What gives you pleasure? Is that pleasure fleeting or forever?
- Death separates us from every source of happiness except Jesus. Can you say with Paul that 'to die is gain' (Philippians 1:21) because Jesus is your ultimate joy?
- What about big life decisions you've made? Your job? Your home? Your relationships? Did you make them on the basis of God's promises for the future?
- What about the decisions you're facing now? What would it mean to make them on the basis of God's promise for the future?

20. THE ADVENTURE OF HOPE

God's new world is a world worth taking risks for. It creates a life of adventure.

In 1812 Adoniram Judson, aged twenty-three, sailed for Burma with the wife he had married just twelve days before. He was the first American overseas missionary. He spent the rest of his life there. This is the letter he had written to Ann Hasseltine's father, asking for her hand in marriage:

> I have now to ask, whether you can consent to part with your daughter early next spring, to see her no more in this world; whether you can consent to her departure, and her subjection to the hardships and sufferings of missionary life; whether you can consent to her exposure to the dangers of the ocean, to the fatal influence of the southern climate of India; to every kind of want and distress; to degradation, insult, persecution, and perhaps a violent death. Can you consent to all this, for the sake of him who left his heavenly home, and died for her and for you; for

> the sake of perishing, immortal souls; for the sake of Zion, and the glory of God? Can you consent to all this, in hope of soon meeting your daughter in the world of glory, with the crown of righteousness, brightened with the acclamations of praise which shall redound to her Saviour from heathens saved, through her means, from eternal woe and despair?[80]

Her father let her decide. She said 'Yes'.

A life of purpose

Christ's death and resurrection give our lives in the present their purpose and meaning.

It seems some people in Corinth were saying there's no resurrection of the dead (1 Corinthians 15:12). So Paul emphasizes that the resurrection of Christ was a real, historic, physical event and Christ's resurrection means that we too will rise.

He also says that, without the resurrection, our lives have no purpose. 'If Christ has not been raised, then our preaching is in vain and your faith is in vain' (14 ESV). The word 'vain' means literally 'empty'. Without the hope of resurrection our lives are empty. 'If Christ has not been raised, your faith is futile; you are still in your sins' (17). Without resurrection, our faith has no basis, our sin has no remedy and our lives have no purpose.

In verse 10, Paul says: 'By the grace of God I am what I am, and his grace toward me was not in vain' (ESV). It's the same phrase: 'in vain'. Paul's life is not in vain. It's not empty. He's the most unworthy apostle for he once persecuted the church of God. But God's grace has given his life purpose, and that purpose is to preach the gospel of salvation in Christ (9–11).

Finally, notice verse 58: 'Therefore, my beloved brothers, be steadfast, immovable, always abounding in the work of the Lord, knowing that in the Lord your labour is not in vain' (ESV). Again it's that same phrase: 'in vain'. This is Paul's application of resurrection truth. Don't give up. Keep going. Work hard. Give yourself. Live for Christ. Live life with purpose. Don't live an empty life.

Robbie Williams, the pop star, said in a television documentary: 'I've got what everybody wants. When I was young and I looked at people like me, I wanted it. But now I've got it all, I'm finding it hard to find any bit of it that I enjoy.' Empty.

An elderly friend of mine met a local businessman who owns a chain of garden centres. 'I'm worth £4 million,' he told my friend. 'But I'm ninety-three, and soon I'll be gone and what will it be worth to me then?' Empty.

I was reading a book in which the author was commenting on the meaninglessness of living to shop. I happened to look out the window to see Bethany Bode cleaning our car. Bethany is a thirteen-year-old girl in our church whose dream is to go to India to serve others on a mission trip when she turns sixteen. In the meantime, she's raising money by doing household chores for people in the church. That's life with meaning. That's a life worth living.

A life of adventure

Paul says: 'I die every day – I mean that, brothers – just as surely as I glory over you in Christ Jesus our Lord. If I fought wild beasts in Ephesus for merely human reasons, what have I gained? If the dead are not raised, "Let us eat and drink, for tomorrow we die"' (31–32).

Let's suppose that Christ has *not* been raised from the dead, says Paul. And so let's suppose there's no life after death. Just suppose. It would make sense to live for this life. Eating and drinking would be the sensible course of action.

Life would have no ultimate meaning, so we should live just for pleasure.

But Paul doesn't believe this and so he doesn't live like that. He's prepared to die daily – to live a life of sacrifice and hard work and service. He's even prepared to face wild beasts. Because life does have a purpose. Because there is resurrection. Some people live for today and die tomorrow. Christians die today and live for tomorrow.

Some people live for today and die tomorrow. Christians die today and live for tomorrow.

Can you see the logic?

- if there's no life after death, then you live for present pleasure
- if there's life after death, then live for eternal reward

What happens when we turn that around?

- if you live for present pleasure, you live as one who *doesn't believe* in resurrection
- if you live for eternal reward, you live as one who *does believe* in resurrection

Paul's life was consistent with his belief in resurrection. People should be able to work out from your life what you believe about the future.

'In your hearts set apart Christ as Lord. Always be prepared to give an answer to everyone who asks you to give the reason for the hope that you have. But do this with gentleness and respect' (1 Peter 3:15). Has anyone asked you recently? Has anyone asked, 'Why do you live like this?

Why did you make that sacrifice? Why didn't you stand up for yourself?' If not, perhaps that's because it looks like you're hoping in the same sort of things that they're hoping in. The true Christian life is about living for something else. It's about having a vision for eternity that makes sacrifice now worthwhile. It's about having confidence for eternity that makes risk now worthwhile. Michael Jensen describes ethics as 'an account of our hopeful lifestyle'. When we act *not* on the basis of any immediate personal benefit, people will wonder what we're doing. It'll seem strange to them. They'll start asking questions. Evangelism just got a whole lot easier!

The present is a moment, the future is forever

> For a thousand years in your sight
> are like a day that has just gone by,
> or like a watch in the night.
> You sweep men away in the sleep of death;
> they are like the new grass of the morning –
> though in the morning it springs up new,
> by evening it is dry and withered.
> (Psalm 90:4–6)

> All men are like grass,
> and all their glory is like the flowers of the field.
> The grass withers and the flowers fall,
> because the breath of the LORD blows on them.
> Surely the people are grass.
> The grass withers and the flowers fall,
> but the word of our God stands for ever.
> (Isaiah 40:6–8)

The whole Bible story is a movement towards the promised future of God. Its underlying premise is that God's future is better than our broken, decaying present. The story is an invitation to look ahead. The promises of God are words about the future that direct our attention forward. Eternity matters more than time. The future age is better than the present age.

Some people suggest that this is dualism, thereby implying that we shouldn't value the future more than the present. There is a dualism which is incompatible with a biblical world-view – the dualism that says that what is mental and spiritual is more important than what is physical or material. But there's another type of dualism that's actually at the heart of a biblical world-view: the priority of the future over the present. 'If your hand or your foot causes you to sin, cut it off and throw it away. It is better for you to enter life maimed or crippled than to have two hands or two feet and be thrown into eternal fire' (Matthew 18:8–9). 'For our light and momentary troubles are achieving for us an eternal glory that far outweighs them all' (2 Corinthians 4:17). 'What matters,' comments Tom Wright, 'is eschatological duality (the present age and the age to come), not ontological duality (an evil 'earth' and a good 'heaven').'[81]

If you're twenty years old, then twenty years is the total amount of time you've experienced. And so a year seems a long time. Twenty, thirty, forty years seem a long time. By the time you're forty, a year is a fortieth of your total experience of time. Half as long. Your life is going to accelerate towards eternity.

Our life is but a moment, a breath. It's the tick of a clock. A blink of an eye. A click of the fingers.

You get one life, once chance. And there's no replay, no rewind.

Don't live for the moment. Live for eternity.

Your suffering and your shame are for a moment. Your reward is forever.

The area in which you live now is for a moment. The location where you spend eternity is forever.

Your temptations and your sin are for a moment. Hell is forever.

Your pride and your achievements are for a moment. God's glory is forever.

Your career is for a moment. God's 'Well done, good and faithful servant' is forever.

Your love life and your sex life are for a moment. Your union with Christ is forever.

Your home now is for a moment. Your home in your heavenly Father's house is forever.

Your money and possessions are for a moment. Your heavenly treasure is forever.

Your pension is for a moment. Your heavenly inheritance is forever.

John Hooper, a Protestant during the reign of Mary Tudor, was facing martyrdom. He was urged by a friend to renounce the faith. 'Life is sweet, death is bitter,' his friend told him. Hooper replied: 'Eternal life is more sweet, eternal death is more bitter.'

Reflect for a moment. Think of the trials you are undergoing. Think of the price you pay to serve Jesus. Think of the price you refuse to pay to serve Jesus. Think of the risks you take. Or don't take. Imagine looking back on this after a million, billion years of eternal glory.

For death and glory

In three separate polls to mark the year 2000, *The Lord of the Rings* by J. R. R. Tolkien was voted the nation's favourite book. The film adaptations, directed by Peter Jackson, are among the top earning films of all time. Part of the appeal of *The Lord of the Rings* is that it contains a sense of moral purpose. It presents a world of valour, honour and courage. In our world, these things have lost their meaning. There are no absolutes, no great truths, no heroic causes. We live in a time when nothing is worth living for, and certainly nothing is worth dying for. We still like the idea of fighting for a great cause, but we're suspicious of great causes – we suspect they're all just power games. A student was asked about a particular military action. 'There's nothing worth dying for,' was her response. Stanley Hauerwas and William H. Willimon comment: 'Which means of course that one day she shall have the unpleasant task of dying for nothing.'[82]

But in *The Lord of the Rings* there is something worth fighting for and dying for. It's what Tolkien's great friend C. S. Lewis called 'a splintered fragment of the true light'. The story of *The Lord of the Rings* mirrors the story of history as the Bible presents it. There is something worth living for and something worth dying for – the rule of Jesus. That rule is *not* the rule of a tyrant, but the rule that sets us free. Here's a great cause that's *not* a power game, because it's the cause of the Lamb. At its heart is the King who died for his people. And that's why it can set us free.

At the end of the film version of *The Two Towers*, Samwise Gamgee, the humble hobbit, the gardener who entered the Fellowship of the Ring by accident, describes how he has come to see that there is something 'worth fighting for':

Sam: Those were the stories that stayed with you – that meant something even if you were too small to understand why. But I think Mr Frodo that I do understand. Folk in those stories had lots of chances of turning back only they didn't. They kept going because they were holding on to something.

Frodo: What are we holding onto, Sam?

Sam: That there is some good in this world. And it's worth fighting for.

There is good and there is evil. These things are not relative. It's not simply a matter of perspective or a manipulation by the powerful. There's something worth fighting for. We see Aragorn and King Théoden mounting their last stand 'for death and glory'. When Jesus explains to his followers what it means to follow the way of the cross, he promises them death and glory (Mark 8:34–38). Here's a cause worth dying for. Here's the promise of eternal glory. Sam says: 'Even darkness must pass. A new day will come. And when the sun shines it will shine out the clearer.'

'I wonder if we'll ever be put into songs and tales,' says Sam as the film closes.

And that's what I'm offering you: a place in the great story, the victory of the Lamb, the ultimate adventure.

CONCLUSION – MY HERO OF THE CROSS AND RESURRECTION

My mother is a hero of the faith. She's not preached to thousands, not planted churches, not written books. But she's a hero of the cross and resurrection.

I tell her story, not because she's unique. Quite the opposite. I think she represents a countless number of ordinary, unsung Christians who live heroic lives. (I'm crying already as I write.) Christians who live quiet lives of sacrifice and service, sustained by living hope. People like the Thessalonians: 'We continually remember before our God and Father your work produced by faith, your labour prompted by love, and your endurance inspired by hope in our Lord Jesus Christ' (1 Thessalonians 1:3). People like my friend Andrew whose daughter's medical condition means he and his wife rarely get to go out. People like the twenty-somethings who've moved onto a needy estate in Sheffield to share the good news of Jesus. People like the young woman who continues serving others in the midst of her depression. People like the couple working only three days a week to create time to serve refugees. You don't have to be a big name to be a hero of the cross and resurrection.

My mother was brought up in a terraced house in Darlington, with two rooms upstairs and two downstairs. The toilet was across the small backyard. The bath was a tin tub in the kitchen. She shared her room with her grandmother. By all accounts, my great-grandmother was a battleaxe. I have a picture of her presiding over a coronation street party – 'presiding' being the word: trenchcoat, grim-faced, in charge. But during much of my mum's childhood, her grandmother was bedridden with gout. Grumpy. Domineering. My mum slept nervously at the foot of her bed. My grandfather worked in the steel mills, routinely coming home with burns up his arms. He was also an alcoholic.

It was a tough life, sustained by the loving strength of my grandmother, 'Nana', as we called her. She was a cheerful woman: compassionate, gentle, uncomplaining. She got on with the life God had given her, living almost all of it in that same house. The second sustaining force in my mother's childhood was the local Methodist church. My Nana attended the church as a babe in arms when it first opened and continued doing so for over ninety years. It was the centre of their lives – their Christian lives and their social lives.

My mother, though, was converted through the youth club of the local Baptist church. She and my father met at a Christian conference. He was a draughtsman, a job long since made obsolete by computers. After their wedding, they moved to London where my father studied at Bible college while my mother worked as a secretary at the Coal Board.

Dad went on to became the pastor of a Baptist church. Mum found herself a pastor's wife, with a set of expectations that ill-matched a working-class girl from a secondary modern school. She also became a young mother, thanks to my arrival on the scene.

I can't calculate the influence she and my father have had on my life. I know I took them for granted as a child. Only when I left home and felt the gap did I realize all that they'd been and done for me while I was growing up. I've never met anyone whose childhood I would have swapped for mine. Love. Security. Encouragement. Godliness. Not just the thousand acts of service, but the constant and consistent love. And the freedom to roam for hours on end in the countryside.

My mother partnered my father in his ministry. She didn't feel able to lead Bible studies or be a counsellor – she was never 'Mrs Pastor'. But she offered endless hospitality. On Sunday mornings we children would always ask, 'Who's coming for dinner today?', because we knew someone would be. She was often left alone, since my father was out in the evenings. We never had much money, but I only realize that now. I always felt rich: loved, secure, well-fed. In a quick-witted family, my mother was always two steps behind, but she never minded. She was able to laugh at herself.

She endured, too, the pressures on my father. The worries of ministries. The frustrations. Sometimes the despair. For several years, we lived in the middle of a building site as the congregation slowly constructed its own new building next to the manse, Saturday morning by Saturday morning. For a small boy, the rubble and trenches were a dream. For a mother, it must have been a nightmare. She loved people, welcomed people, served people. Extolled Christ. And she prayed. Above all, her warm, compassionate smile made countless people feel like they belonged. And she never complained.

For the last fifteen or so years, my mother has had acute

arthritis. Her hands have curled over and her body is riddled with pain. Each week she goes to hospital for gold injections. In many ways, the condition has come to dominate her life and yet it doesn't define her. People ask me how she's doing and I struggle to remember they're asking about her arthritis! It's never been a feature of her conversation. She doesn't make a fuss, doesn't want to be the centre of attention. Social situations leave her exhausted, but you wouldn't know it at the time. Plus, in my mind she is still the graceful, caring woman I knew as a child. And still she never complains.

These are not just the words of a dutiful son. More people than I can count have said to me, 'Your mother's so lovely.' Only yesterday, a young woman said to me, 'I do love your mother.' Her achievements will never be listed in history books. But everywhere she goes she brings the sweet savour of Jesus. Perhaps even more so in her suffering.

She bears it all with grace. She is content. Her heart is still quick to serve, even if her body is slower. She doesn't fear death. I've lost count of the number of hymns she's told me she wants at her funeral. All rousing hymns of joy in Christ. If we sing them all, we'll go on well into the night!

She loves her Saviour. She's expected little from life and received every blessing as a bonus. She's served without hesitation, suffered without complaint. Her life has been shaped by the cross. Her future will be shaped by the resurrection. She's my hero of the cross and resurrection.

Her life has been shaped by the cross. Her future will be shaped by the resurrection.

NOTES

Chapter 3 Humility

1 George Barna, *Growing True Disciples*, WaterBrook Press, 2001, pp. 67–68, 77.
2 Cited in Duncan B. Forrester, *On Human Worth: A Christian Vindication of Equality*, SCM, 2001, p. 115.
3 C. S. Lewis, *The Screwtape Letters*, Geoffrey Bles, 1942, pp. 71–72.
4 Ibid., pp. 72–73.
5 John Owen, 'On Indwelling Sin', in *Overcoming Sin and Temptation*, eds. Kelly M. Kapic and Justin Taylor, Crossway, 2006, p. 282.
6 Cited in C. J. Mahaney, *Humility: True Greatness*, Multnomah, 2005, p. 66.
7 John Stott, *The Message of Galatians*, IVP, 1968, p. 179.

Chapter 4 Confidence

8 Terry Virgo, *God's Lavish Grace*, Monarch, 2004, pp. 34–35.
9 John Stott, *What Christ Thinks of the Church*, Monarch, 2003, p. 33.
10 John Owen, *Communion with God*, abridged by R. J. K. Law, Banner of Truth, 1991, pp. 16, 17, 32–33.

Chapter 5 The way of Jesus = the way of the cross

11 Michael J. Gorman, *Cruciformity: Paul's Narrative Spirituality of the Cross*, Eerdmans, 2001, pp. 4, 173.
12 Stanley Hauerwas and William H. Willimon, *Resident Aliens: Life in the Christian Colony*, Abingdon, 1989, p. 47.

13 Michael J. Gorman, *Cruciformity: Paul's Narrative Spirituality of the Cross*, Eerdmans, 2001, p. 30.

14 David Garrison, *Church Planting Movements,* www.imb.org/cpm, 1999.

15 Dietrich Bonhoeffer, *The Cost of Discipleship,* trans. R. H. Fuller, SCM, 1937, 1959, pp. 79–80.

Chapter 6 Everyday martyrdom

16 Michael J. Gorman, *Cruciformity: Paul's Narrative Spirituality of the Cross*, Eerdmans, 2001, p. 92.

17 Cited in Michael J. Gorman, *Cruciformity*, p. 5.

Chapter 7 The value of Jesus

18 John Piper, *Don't Waste Your Life*, Crossway, 2003.

19 Ibid., p. 10.

20 Ibid., pp. 45–46.

21 Ibid., p. 76.

22 Emir Fethi Caner and H. Edward Pruitt, *The Costly Call*, Kregel, 2005, p. 96.

Chapter 8 The way of the cross = the way of joy

23 David F. Wells, *Above All Earthly Pow'rs: Christ in a Postmodern World*, IVP/Eerdmans, 2005, pp. 48–52.

24 David W. Henderson, *Culture Shift*, Baker, 1998, pp. 29–30.

25 Meic Pearse, 'Growing Up Is Hard To Do', *EG* 20, LICC, October 2008, p. 5.

26 Michael J. Gorman, *Cruciformity: Paul's Narrative Spirituality of the Cross*, Eerdmans, 2001, p. 389.

27 Paul David Tripp, *A Quest for More*, New Growth Press, 2008, p. 44.

28 Ibid., pp. 18–19.

29 Dietrich Bonhoeffer, *The Cost of Discipleship,* trans. R. H. Fuller, SCM, 1937, 1959, pp. 77–78.

Chapter 9 No glory without the cross

30 Dietrich Bonhoeffer, *The Cost of Discipleship*, trans. R. H. Fuller, SCM, 1937, 1959, p. 77.

Chapter 10 Bondage followed by liberation

31 Karl Barth, *Church Dogmatics* 4.1, cited in Alister McGrath, *Christian Theology: An Introduction*, Blackwell, 1994, p. 354.

32 Alister McGrath, *The Enigma of the Cross*, Hodder and Stoughton, 1987, p. 32.

33 Meic Pearse, 'Growing Up Is Hard To Do', *EG* 20, LICC, October 2008, p. 4.

34 Tony Campolo, *It's Friday, but Sunday's Comin'*, Word, 1985, pp. 124–126.

Chapter 11 Hiddenness followed by revelation

35 See also Matthew 10:26; 24:30; Mark 4:22; Luke 8:17; 12:2; Romans 2:5; 8:18–19; 1 Timothy 6:14; Titus 2:13; 1 Peter 1:13; 4:13; 5:1, 4; 1 John 3:2.

36 John Calvin, *Calvin's Commentaries: The Second Epistle of Paul the Apostle to the Corinthians and the Epistles to Timothy, Titus and Philemon*, trans. T. A. Smail, St Andrew Press, 1964, pp. 332–333.

37 Adapted from Tim Chester, 'Christ's Little Flock: Towards an Ecclesiology of the Cross', *Evangel* 19:1, Spring 2001, pp. 13–21. For the political implications of the pattern of the cross and resurrection, see Tim Chester, *Good News to the Poor*, IVP, 2004, especially chapters 10–11.

38 David W. Smith, *Against the Stream: Christianity and Mission in an Age of Globalization*, IVP, 2003, p. 123.

39 Don Carson, cited in Derek Tidball, *The Message of the Cross*, IVP, 2001, pp. 213–214.

40 *Luther's Works* Vol. 51, pp. 76–77, cited in Mark D. Thompson, 'Martin Luther: A Theologian Forged by Trial', *On Eagles' Wings: An Exploration of Strength in the Midst of Weakness*,

eds. Michael Parson and David J. Cohen, Wipf and Stock, p. 102.

41 Mark D. Thompson, 'Martin Luther: A Theologian Forged by Trial', p. 104.

42 Samuel Escobar, *Christian Mission in a New Century*, IVP, 2003, p. 24.

43 See Martin Luther, 'The Heidelberg Disputation', *Luther: Early Theological Works*, Library of Christian Classics Vol. XVI, SCM/Westminster, 1962, pp. 274–307; Tim Chester and Steve Timmis, *Total Church*, IVP/Crossway, 2007/2008, pp. 165–167; Alister McGrath, *Luther's Theology of the Cross*, Blackwell, 1985; and Graham Tomlin, *The Power of the Cross: Theology and the Death of Christ in Paul, Luther and Pascal*, Paternoster, 1999.

44 See Emil Brunner, *The Mediator*, Lutterworth, 1934, p. 435.

45 '*tectum sub cruce et sub contrario*'; cited in Jürgen Moltmann, *Theology of Hope*, trans. James. W. Leitch, SCM, 1965, ET 1967, p. 223.

Chapter 12 Suffering followed by glory

46 Richard Bauckham, 'Weakness – Paul' s and Ours', *Themelios* 7.3, 1982, p. 5.

47 See Tim Chester, *Good News to the Poor*, IVP, 2003, chapter 11 and Tim Chester and Steve Timmis, *Total Church*, IVP/Crossway, 2007/2008, chapter 13.

48 John Calvin, *Calvin's Commentaries: A Harmony of the Gospels Matthew, Mark and Luke Vol. III*, trans. A. W. Morrison, St Andrew Press, 1972, pp. 72–73.

49 John Calvin, *The Institutes of Christian Religion*, trans. F. L. Battles, ed. J. T. McNeill, Westminster/SCM, 1961, 3.2.42.

50 John Calvin, *Calvin's Commentaries: Hebrews and 1 & 2 Peter*, trans. William B. Johnston, St Andrew Press, 1963, pp. 157–158.

51 Betty Carlson, *A Song and a Prayer: Devotional Thoughts from L'Abri*, Hodder and Stoughton, 1970, pp. 65–66.

Chapter 13 Resurrection power, freedom and life

52 Peter Hicks, *The Message of Evil and Suffering*, IVP, 2006, p. 91.

53 Tom Wright, *Surprised by Hope*, SPCK, 2007, p. 262.

54 Adapted from Tim Chester, 'Eschatology and Mission: The Kingdom of God is at Hand', *What Are We Waiting For? Christian Hope and Contemporary Culture*, eds. Stephen Holmes and Russell Rook, Paternoster, 2008, pp. 87–97.

55 Christopher J. H. Wright, *The Mission of God: Unlocking the Bible's Grand Narrative*, IVP, 2006.

56 For an example of an evangelistic course that follows the Bible story, see Tim Chester and Steve Timmis, *The World We All Want*, Authentic, 2005.

Chapter 14 Power to be weak

57 Alister McGrath, *The Enigma of the Cross*, Hodder and Stoughton, 1987, p. 30.

58 Derek Tidball, *The Message of the Cross*, IVP, 2001, p. 214.

59 Richard Mouw, *Politics and the Biblical Drama*, Baker, 1976, p. 41.

60 Graham Tomlin, *The Power of the Cross: Theology and the Death of Christ in Paul, Luther and Pascal*, Paternoster, 1999, p. 313.

61 Evelyn Ashley, 'The Scandal of Weak Leadership', *On Eagles' Wings: An Exploration of Strength in the Midst of Weakness*, eds. Michael Parson and David J. Cohen, Wipf and Stock, 2008, p. 74.

62 Cited by Mark D. Thompson, 'Martin Luther: A Theologian Forged by Trial', *On Eagles' Wings: An Exploration of Strength in the Midst of Weakness*, eds. Michael Parson and David J. Cohen, Wipf and Stock, 2008, p.104.

63 See 1 Corinthians 2:1–5; 4:1–5; 8:1–3; 9:7–18; 13:1–7; 2 Corinthians 10:1, 10–18; 11:5–12, 30; 12:7–18; 13:4, 9–10.

Chapter 15 Freedom to serve, life to die

64 Michael J. Gorman, *Cruciformity: Paul's Narrative Spirituality of the Cross*, Eerdmans, 2001, pp. 91, 186–188, 192–193, 197, 230–244, 252.

Chapter 16 The Spirit of resurrection

65 Gordon Fee, *Paul, the Spirit and the People of God*, Hodder & Stoughton, 1997, p. 49.
66 Michael J. Gorman, *Cruciformity: Paul's Narrative Spirituality of the Cross*, Eerdmans, 2001, pp. 52, 60.

Chapter 17 A renewed world of life

67 Tom Wright, *Surprised by Hope*, SPCK, 2007, p. 164.
68 Andrew T. Lincoln, *Paradise Now and Not Yet*, Baker, 1981, p. 193.
69 Martyn Lloyd-Jones, *The Final Perseverance of the Saints: Romans 8:17–39*, Banner of Truth, 1975, pp. 86, 88–89.
70 Tom Wright, *Surprised by Hope*, SPCK, 2007, p. 126.
71 Ibid., p. 168.

Chapter 18 A world of justice, joy and love

72 C. S. Lewis, *The Problem of Pain*, Macmillan, 1962, p. 145.
73 G. K. Chesterton, 'The Ethics of Elfland', *Orthodoxy*, House of Stratus, 2001, p. 41.
74 Jonathan Edwards, *Charity and Its Fruits*, Banner of Truth, 1852, 1969, pp. 321–368.
75 Rephrased in more contemporary English from Jonathan Edwards, *Charity and Its Fruits*, pp. 352–353.

Chapter 19 A world worth living for and a world worth dying for

76 Shane Claiborne and Jonathan Wilson-Hartgrove, *Becoming the Answer to Our Prayers: Prayers for Ordinary Radicals*, IVP, 2008, p. 53.

77 Paul David Tripp, *A Quest for More*, New Growth Press, 2008, p. 180.

78 Francis Schaeffer, 'Ash Heap Lives', available online. (Originally published in Francis Schaeffer, *Ash Heap Lives*, Norfolk Press, 1975.)

79 John Calvin, *Calvin's Commentaries: The Epistles of Paul the Apostle to the Romans and to the Thessalonians*, trans. Ross Mackenzie, St Andrew Press, 1961, p. 335.

Chapter 20 The adventure of hope

80 Courtney Anderson, *To the Golden Shore: The Life of Adoniram Judson*, Zondervan, 1956, p. 83; cited in John Piper, *Don't Waste Your Life*, Crossway, 2003, p. 158.

81 Tom Wright, *Surprised by Hope*, SPCK, 2007, p. 106.

82 Stanley Hauerwas and William H. Willimon, *Resident Aliens: Life in the Christian Colony*, Abingdon, 1989, pp. 149–150.

also by Tim Chester

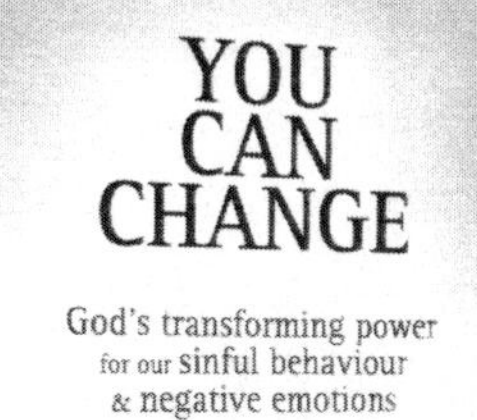

... you don't have to be stuck in a sinning rut!

Other books describe how we should live, but this book outlines how we can change. It's about hope: the hope we have in Jesus, hope for forgiveness, and hope for real and lasting change. God promises liberating grace and transforming power to his people.

The author points to Jesus and explains how faith in him can lead to change. Biblical, accessible and practical, this book also offers change projects for those who are serious about becoming more like Jesus and less like their old selves.

'Many books are written by experts. This book isn't one of them,' admits Tim Chester. *'It was written out of my own struggle to change. My long battle with particular issues set me searching the Bible as well as writings from the past. This book shares the amazing truths I discovered that now give me hope.'*

'For years I wondered if I'd ever overcome certain sins. And while I can't claim to have conquered sin – for no-one ever can do – here are discoveries that have led to change in my life and in the lives of others.'

ISBN:
978-1-84474-303-2

Available from your local Christian bookshop or via our website at **www.ivpbooks.com**

also by Tim Chester

Total Church
Tim Chester & Steve Timmis
978-1-84474-191-5

How does your church measure up?

Total Church pleads for two key principles for church and mission: the gospel as content, and the community as context.

The authors call for us to be word- and mission-centred (for the gospel is truth to be proclaimed) as we share our lives as Christians and offer a place of belonging to unbelievers.

The Busy Christian's Guide to Busyness 978–1-84474-302–5

Do you say 'yes' when really you mean 'no'? Do you feel trapped by your 24/7 lifestyle?

Tim Chester offers practical help to busy Christians, but also opts for root-and-branch treatment: you need to deal radically with the things that are driving you.

God has promised his rest to all who are weary and burdened (Matthew 11:28). It's up to us to accept it.